The Gift of Wealth

Time-Tested Strategies to Build, Protect and Preserve Wealth

A lifetime collection of personal experiences, and a compilation of teachings from respected experts in personal financial matters.

Based on the concepts of attaining financial security and independence in a long – but ultimately short – way.

Asher Lieblich
CPA, CFP®, MBA

Copyright © 2015 by Asher Lieblich. All rights reserved.
www.lfswealth.com

No part of this publication may be reproduced, stored in a retrieval system, or transmitted in any form or by any means, electronic, mechanical, photocopying, recording, scanning, or otherwise, except as permitted under Section 107 or 108 of the 1976 United States Copyright Act, without the prior written permission of the Publisher. Requests to the author for permission should be addressed to Asher Lieblich, 565 Montgomery Street, Brooklyn, NY 11225, (718) 771-0887, fax (347) 765-1562, or to asher@lfswealth.com.

Limit of Liability/Disclaimer of Warranty: While the author used his best efforts in preparing this book, he makes no representations or warranties with respect to the accuracy or completeness of the contents of this book and specifically disclaim any implied warranties or merchant-ability or fitness for a particular service. No warranty may be created or extended by sales representatives or written sales materials. The advice and strategies contained herein may not be suitable for your situation. You should consult with a professional where appropriate. The author shall not be liable for any loss of profit or any other commercial damages, including but not limited to special, incidental, consequential, or other damages.

As of the time of writing, Asher Lieblich is an advisor with H.D. Vest Investment Services[SM]. The views and opinions presented in this book are those of Asher Lieblich and not of H.D. Vest Financial Services® or its subsidiaries. All investment-related information in this book is for informational purposes only and does not constitute a solicitation or offer to sell securities or insurance services. H.D. Vest Financial Services® is the holding company for the group of companies providing financial services under the H.D. Vest name.

Securities offered through H.D. Vest Investment Services[SM], Member: SIPC; Advisory Services offered through H.D. Vest Advisory Services[SM], 6333 North State Highway 161, Fourth Floor, Irving, TX 75038, 972-870-6000. Investments and Insurance Products are not insured by the FDIC or any federal government agency. They are not deposits of, or guaranteed by, the bank or any bank affiliate, and they may lose value.

Lieblich Financial Services is not a registered broker/dealer or independent investment advisory firm.

Printed in the United States of America

ISBN 978-1512269154

Cover Design: Moshe Danzinger

Author's notes:

The names, details, and circumstances may have been changed to protect the privacy of those mentioned in this publication.

To facilitate a smoother reading of the text, we have opted to use the generic "he" and "his" to refer to both male and female.

About the Title Page

A Talmudic Tale

Rabbi Yehoshua relates:

Once, as I was walking down a road, I saw a little boy sitting by a fork in the road.

I asked him, "My son, which road leads to the city?"

"Both roads lead to the city," he answered me.

"And which is the shorter?" I asked.

"This road is a short road but a long one," and pointing to the other road, said, "that one is a long road, and at the same time a short one."

I went down the road which the boy said was short and at the same time long.

On approaching the city, I found it surrounded by gardens and orchards that blocked its entrance to such an extent that I had to return to the place from which I started.

The boy was still sitting beside the road so I asked him, "My son, didn't you say that this road was the shorter one?"

"Yes, Rabbi," he replied, "but did I not also tell you that it was, at the same time, the longer one?"

The Rabbi kissed him on the head and said: "Praiseworthy are you O Israel, for you are all very wise, from your oldest to your young."

–*Talmud, Eruvin* 53b

Implementing a plan using time-tested strategies for the accumulation of wealth avoids the risk of having to "retrace one's steps" to rebuild wealth lost through lack of planning. To build, protect, and preserve wealth, take the long (i.e., tried and tested) – but ultimately short – way.

*This book is dedicated
in memory of my mother,
Rivka Yehudith Lieblich,
for the sacrifices and commitment
she made throughout her life
to provide her children with the opportunity
to live a productive, family-centered life!*

TABLE OF CONTENTS

THE GIFT OF WEALTH

PREFACE xi
ACKNOWLEDGMENTS xv
INTRODUCTION xix
   Realizations From Life on a Kibbutz xxi
      My father's influence xxii
AUTHOR'S FOREWORD xxv
   Save or Spend? Diet or Splurge? It's All Up to You xxvii
      Principles of healthy living xxvii
      Maimonides' guarantee xxviii
      Maimonides' 10 principles of well-being xxviii
      10 principles of successful investing xxx

Chapter 1 AN INTRODUCTION TO INVESTING 1
   America's Wealth 3
   Investment Glossary 7
   Simplicity Is the Ultimate Sophistication... "The Rest Is Commentary" .. 12
      Profoundly "simple" advice 16
   The Foundation for Successful Living 17
      Marriage and finance 17
      Develop a strategy and stick with it: Comparing
        marriage and investment strategies 17

Chapter 2 THE IMPORTANCE OF A FINANCIAL COACH 21
   All You Need Is Information.... Really? 23
      Does information equal wisdom? 24
      Don't ask for the bell when what you really want is the dinner 26
      Dalbar's Quantitative Analysis of Investor Behavior 28
      Emotional Cycle of Investing 29
   A Financial Advisor 30
      Accepting professional guidance 32
      What is the role of a financial advisor? 33
      An offer from the bank officer: two tales 34

| VII

An investor who was not so fortunate	35
The Trusted Advisor	36
Telling the truth	37
"How can we trust you?"	39
Chapter 3 MOVING FORWARD	43
The End Result Begins With a Plan	45
If you have no idea where you are going, any road will get you there	46
Goals and objectives	47
A goal without a plan is just a wish	48
Setting goals	49
Expectations regarding returns	51
Measure your returns against your benchmark	52
Do not lose money	52
Most important is to take action	53
Investment Time Horizon	54
The Right (and Wrong) Way to Invest	57
The First Step: Understanding Risk	61
Risk tolerance	62
Risk capacity	63
Balancing risk	63
Financial market risks	65
Other important terms	67
Although you cannot avoid risk, you can learn to manage it	71
Personal financial risks – A short questionnaire	72
Controlling your personal risks	73
Asset Allocation	74
The famous musician	74
A symphonic portfolio	75
Identifying possible "instruments" in a diversified portfolio	77
A helpful warning	78
Rebalancing to Remain on Course	79
Considerations in rebalancing a portfolio	81
Discipline a must	82
Investor Behavior	82
Listening to the one who knows better: The fur dealer and the Rebbe	83
The Mind Rules the Heart	85
The tale of the cat and mouse	85
Sammy and the Middle East Crisis	91
How to Buy Mutual Funds	93
Is a mutual fund track record useful?	95

Individual Stocks: Serious Business or Social Investing? 97
    When to sell a stock 99
        Investing in stocks: half a transaction is not enough 102
Why You Should Not invest in Individual Stocks 103

Chapter 4   **RETIREMENT PLANNING** 109
    The Need for Retirement Planning: An Introduction 111
    Accumulation: Paying Yourself First 116
        Always! 117
        When money is saved and invested, you don't spend it 119
    Distribution in Retirement and the 4% Rule 120
        A Goal of Maintaining Financial Independence
          and Dignity in Retirement 120
    Sequence of Returns 124
    The Investment Plan 126
    Managing Uncle Sam, Your Tax Partner 136

Chapter 5   **CLOSING THOUGHTS** 141
    The Good That Financial Advisors Do 143
    A Final Thought 145

APPENDICES
    Appendix A: **Letting the Fox Divide the Sheep** 149
    Appendix B: **Risk Profile Questionnaire** 153
    Appendix C: **Definitions** 161
    Appendix D: **Recommended Reading** 165

About the Author 167

Preface

The following message was left on my telephone voicemail:

"Asher, this is Steve. I need that letter. I spoke to Marian and she told me that the bank thinks I don't want the loan. I, I must have that letter. It's been two weeks. If ... I don't get the letter I may...."

The tension in his voice was palpable. Listening to the message, I could sense the intense pressure he was under. He was desperate.

Steve, a successful self-employed attorney, was financially insolvent. Despite a yearly income in excess of $500,000, he was delinquent on his tax payments and was about to default on his home mortgage. Steve and his wife were living the "high life" and their spending was way beyond their means. Their dining and entertainment expenses were greater than the average American worker's wages, and his wife didn't think twice about spending $4,000 on a dress she happened to see in the mall for their 7-year-old daughter.

Over the years, I tried without success to encourage him and his wife to moderate their spending. Now he was desperate and had to refinance his home mortgage to raise money for his immediate expenses. He called me asking for a letter to the bank verifying his income and his financial assets, a letter usually required by banks in the case of self-employed individuals. I was away from the office when he called and left the voicemail message shown above.

A few days prior to receiving the telephone message from Steve, a recently retired 65-year-old woman, Yvonne, was referred to me by one of my clients. I prepared her rather simple tax return involving only modest wages and some interest and dividend income. After I completed her tax return, our next discussion shifted to her plans to retire. She asked me if I wouldn't mind looking at her brokerage account statements and advise her on a strategy to generate income from her portfolio that would last her lifetime.

She had two accounts: an Individual Retirement Account (IRA) and a regular account. The thought that went through my mind was, "How much can she have already?" In her last year of working, her wages were the highest ever, about $36,000. To my great surprise, her combined portfolios had a market value of close to $2 million.

"WOW!" was the first thought that entered my mind, and I immediately asked her, "How were you able to accumulate such a portfolio?"

"You see, Mr. Lieblich," she replied, "I started working when I was 18 years old, making about $75 a week. I never had any money before that, and I spent everything I made. But after a few months I realized that I had nothing to show for my money. I felt that my work was for nothing. So I decided that I would save 10% of my salary every week. But I didn't know what to do with the money or where to put it, so I asked my boss what he does with his savings. He told me that he invests in the stock market, and he'd tell me how to invest. So every month I just kept buying stocks and mutual funds. I never sold.

"But Mr. Lieblich," she continued, "now that I am retired, do you think I have enough to live on for the rest of my life? Both my parents lived to their nineties." Despite her success in accumulating a sizeable portfolio, she felt she needed guidance as she entered a new stage in her life – retirement – where she would need to ensure that her investments would sustain her for the long term as she withdraws funds.

When I returned to my office a few days later, I received a telephone call from Tom, Steve's brother-in-law, informing me that Steve had been killed in a car accident just two days before. He was speaking on his cell phone when he went through a red light and was hit by a truck. He was killed instantly. The date and time of his death were the same as the voicemail message he left me. Those were his final words and, having never erased that message, I often listen to it. His urgency and intensity were tangible, and I shudder at the desperate state of mind he must have been in. What is sadder is that with his high income, none of this had to happen.

Steve's and Yvonne's paths in life couldn't have been more dissimilar: Steve for his unfortunate financial path and Yvonne for her intuitive wisdom. As I reflected on these two stories, and being a Certified Public Accountant and a Certified Financial Planner, I felt I had an obligation to educate the public on financial matters. I could see that the way a person managed his finances was more than a science or a gamble. In some cases it was a blessing, and in others a matter of life or death. A few weeks after Steve's tragic death and my experience with Yvonne, I was approached by an organization to deliver a lecture on personal finance to a group of Russian immigrants. As is true of most people, public speaking was a terrifying activity for me, but because of my widened experience with both clients, I accepted for the first time and have delivered numerous talks about this subject since then.

This book is a result of my experiences with Steve and Yvonne and many other clients over the course of my forty-year career. I came to the realization that many people, especially young married couples, are not properly prepared to deal with the many issues they face regarding their personal finances. It was essential for me that my children (and grandchildren) conduct their personal financial lives in a prudent and responsible manner.

The Richest Man in Babylon, written in the 1920s, is a wonderful book that provides great tips on how to manage money while providing guidance for a prosperous life. I gave my children financial incentives to read the book and all benefited from its wisdom.

My involvement in the financial services profession, however, provided me with further insights that I wished to share with my children; insights that would enhance their understanding of investments and money management.

The financial industry has evolved since the 1920s, and a message with modern themes and examples would further deepen their knowledge. My initial intention was to write a memo to my children to serve as a guide, but as I gathered material and began writing, the intended memo expanded to this book with a mission to provide clarity in personal financial and investment decisions.

Asher Lieblich

Acknowledgments

I am very fortunate that both my parents and my in-laws provided me with invaluable guideposts for a successful livelihood as a Certified Public Accountant and a Certified Financial Planner,™ along with their encouragement to share my experience and knowledge with others.

My mother, Rivka Yehudith bas Asher Anshel, of blessed memory, a true woman of valor, endured many hardships and was nevertheless a source of optimism: she imbued her children with many good qualities, and particularly the importance of family harmony.

My father, Abraham Lieblich, set an example through his hard work and self-sacrifice for the family, of how to plan for the future and conduct oneself in an ethical and decent manner in business and personal life.

My mother-in-law, Miriam bas Moshe, of blessed memory, the antithesis of every mother-in-law joke, was a quiet, gentle and unassuming person. But her wisdom ran deep. She never interfered but always offered the wisest advice when asked.

My father-in-law, Israel Plotnick, is beloved by everyone who is fortunate enough to meet him. His mission in life is, as he often told me, "to help others," and he truly lives by that maxim. I learned how to budget my finances from him. In addition, his love for the stock market was contagious and his stock-trading activities taught me valuable lessons when we were both younger.

I am very grateful to the staff at HD Vest Financial Services organization and its President and CEO Roger Ochs, who always emphasizes that our primary responsibility is to serve our clients and help them pursue their financial goals.

I would like to thank my staff at Lieblich Financial Services: Sara Mayteles, Moshe Danzinger, David Lieblich, Devorah Salek and Malka Laskey. They have always supported me when I've been in need of help, and have kept the accounting and financial services practice running smoothly. Moshe is particularly helpful in performing computer and graphic design work.

This book is a collection of experiences and concepts I learned over forty years in the financial industry. Some are original and some are borrowed. Where possible, I have acknowledged the source. However, as a voracious reader, I have read numerous books and other publications, and frequently attend professional conferences, and cannot possibly identify all the sources of those who shaped my thinking.

Special thanks to Chana Shloush for taking my numerous notes and thoughts and compiling them into readable material, and to Rochel Chana Riven for helping me transform the manuscript into a professionally written book while preserving my voice and making the book flow.

My relationship with Rabbi Shloma Majeski is unique; he is a friend and an inspiring mentor. His contributions are interwoven throughout the book and include stories and the lessons to be learned from them. Financial matters tend to be dry, and his colorful and wise additions add much sparkle to the book.

Finally, I would like to acknowledge and thank my wife, Chaya Sara, a synthesis of the great qualities of her father and mother. At my side for forty years, you made it possible for me to do the work I love, while managing to raise our wonderful children almost single-handedly. As my partner, your *chessed* (good deeds) and generosity in helping others is inspiring, and I attribute my achievements in business largely as Heaven's reward for your activities.

*With wisdom,
one's rooms will be filled with
all kinds of precious and pleasant wealth.*

– *Mishlei (Proverbs)* 24:4

INTRODUCTION

REALIZATIONS FROM LIFE ON A KIBBUTZ

"Asher, get down!"

Someone was shooting at us. Chaim was calling out to me as the searing, buzzing noise whizzed close to my head. I looked around and saw Chaim lying on the rocky ground, his hands covering his head. I immediately followed suit, falling to the ground and assuming that same position. In that instant, I recalled the advice my father-in-law gave to me and my new bride just before we moved to Israel. As a former soldier himself, he had learned that the moment one heard a sound even remotely resembling a bullet or bomb, he should not look around for its source but immediately fall to the ground, cover his head, and wait until the noise stops. With that in mind, I lay on the ground next to Chaim for a few moments until, sure enough, the shooting stopped.

What led up to this gripping incident was my wife's and my decision shortly after our wedding to immigrate to Israel and make a difference in the world. Being idealistic, we volunteered to work in a *kibbutz* in Israel. Ours was an agricultural *kibbutz* with a stable of horses. Its members also raised cattle for the beef market, and grew oranges and cotton. My job was to feed and care for the cows. At the time of the incident, Chaim and I were on a hilltop searching for a missing cow. Our cows were grazing in fields adjacent to the *kibbutz* in the Ayalon Valley, and our pastures were surrounded by fences. A Bedouin tribe was encamped nearby and they would often cut the fence and bring their sheep and goats to graze on our private land.

We immediately made our way back to the *kibbutz* (on a tractor) and reported the incident, but the culprits were never found.

My wife was pregnant with our first daughter while we attempted to adapt to the *kibbutz* lifestyle. Now, a *kibbutz* is a community with shared ideals and shared income. All the money earned by its various enterprises is pooled together. Everybody receives the same-sized apartment and a very modest monthly stipend depending on family size. Everyone eats in a central dining room, and the children, six weeks and older, are placed in a communal daycare center so that the mother can join the workforce. After a few months, I realized that such a lifestyle did not suit me as I am a highly self-motivated entrepreneur by nature and want to be personally rewarded for my hard work. The birth of our newborn daughter sealed our decision since my wife refused to part with Yael and place her in a daycare center at such a young age. Thus, we decided to move back to the United States where I would pursue my dream of having my own business.

Reminiscent of the fall of communism, a short time later the *kibbutz* itself was dissolved and the various agricultural and animal farming enterprises were distributed to the members. Community sharing is a wonderful, idealistic goal, but in my view, it is unworkable in the long run. The hard-working, motivated individuals eventually begrudge those who are not carrying their fair share of the work load yet benefit equally with those who produce the most.

My father's influence

My father was a major influence in shaping my values and attitudes toward investing. Having spent his youth as a slave laborer in various German concentration camps, he learned early on that in order to survive, he would have to plan how and when to consume his meager daily food portion. Each man received one slice of bread at night after work. While most men quickly ate the entire slice, my father ate only half and saved the rest for the morning.

After the war, my parents immigrated to Israel where my father first worked on a *kibbutz* as a machinist. Money was tight, so in order to improve our family's finances, he found a better-paying job in the mines by the Dead Sea. The downside to this job were the over-100 degree temperatures even in the winter, and the fact that he came home just once every two weeks.

After working for seven years at this grueling job, my father decided to seek a better life, so he moved the family to the U.S. where he again worked as a machinist in a factory. He always maintained the good habits of his youth, and his way of life was distinguished by saving as much of his hard-earned money as possible and living within his means throughout his working days. He retired to a comfortable lifestyle while, ironically, many of his friends who had earned significantly more than he did but did not plan appropriately during their working years, struggle today in retirement.

My father is a great role model for me on how to live life. As I watched him struggle during the tough years, it became apparent to me that his values were clear and well-defined. Taking care of our family was his number one priority. My brothers and I never felt deprived of any of our basic material needs. His other priority was to live always within his means and manage to save for the future.

I know I am telling you a great deal about my father, and you may wonder what this has to do with my approach to financial planning. Simply put, my father's experiences left a significant mark on me. It engendered in me a passion to work with families to help them pursue financial peace of mind. If I could – through thoughtful financial planning – help people increase their wealth and assist them in protecting what they have and maintaining sustainable income, that would give me great satisfaction. Today my business has a simple mission: to help families build and protect their wealth and, in retirement, maintain their dignity and independence.

As I wrote this book, I had in mind that the sound and sage advice I had received from my father be passed on to my children so that they, too, would conduct their financial affairs responsibly.

The following story illustrates how the examples that my wife and I try to model for our children had their desired effect. During a family vacation to Orlando, Florida, we visited an upscale, world-renowned toy store. My children were wandering around the store looking at the toys and dolls and I noticed my daughter Malka, who was eight years old at the time, looking carefully at a rack with dolls. I was hoping that she wouldn't ask me to buy a doll because I knew that I would definitely refuse. The lowest-priced dolls were over $125, and some toys were priced over $4,000.

Malka came over to me and in a very low, almost conspiratorial, voice said, "Tatty, can I ask you a question?" I followed her to a quiet corner and she said, "Aren't they embarrassed to charge so much?"

Author's Foreword

SAVE OR SPEND? DIET OR SPLURGE? IT'S ALL UP TO YOU

Principles of healthy living

Walk into a typical bookstore and you'll notice that the two largest sections are books about dieting and personal finance. Almost every one of these books claims either to help you lose weight quickly or become wealthy fast.

When it comes to your diet, it is simply a choice between broccoli and chocolate cake. Broccoli is good for you, while chocolate cake only tastes good. But when you're sitting down to dinner with friends or at a party and you're faced with this choice, your mind tells you to reach for the broccoli but the desire for pleasure tells you to go for the cake. So you eat the cake and live with the consequences.

The same can be said for your money. You know you have to live within your means: to save, as well as to plan for your future, your children's education, and your retirement. But at the moment of truth, when faced with the desire to buy a new watch, a new outfit, or a new car on impulse, or save your money for the future, you spend the money and put off the saving.

What we choose to eat and what we choose to save are the paramount choices in our lives, and more often than not we make the wrong decisions (i.e., instant gratification wins and we "choose the cake" or "buy the watch"). We wind up having to open our belts another notch after every meal and having an empty wallet soon after every payday.

In the following two sections, we will compare the importance of a healthy diet with a healthy plan for one's finances.

Maimonides' guarantee

One of the greatest Jewish philosophers, Talmudic scholars, and physicians of the Middle Ages, Moshe ben Maimon (also known as Rambam or Maimonides) had many wise words regarding the benefits of healthful eating. Follow his ten simple rules, he said, and you will be healthy throughout your lifetime.

A doctor by profession, he reached the peak of his professional career as the royal physician in Saladin's Egyptian court. Today, many hospitals and schools around the world are named after him. The *Mishneh Torah*, his 14-volume compilation of Jewish law, established him as the leading rabbinic authority of his time, and possibly of all time.

Though the *Mishneh Torah* is a compilation of Jewish laws, Rambam reasoned that to serve G-d, a person needs a healthy mind as well as a healthy body. He devoted a section in the *Mishneh Torah* to a person's physical well-being and provided specific advice. So certain was Rambam of his recommendations on living a healthy life that he gave the following guarantee:

"For those who follow these principles, I guarantee that their lives will be free from disease, they will never need a doctor, and they will be healthy throughout their lifetime" (Hilchos Deos 4:20).

Maimonides' 10 principles of well-being

1) Since a healthy body is necessary in leading a fulfilling life, you should separate yourself from harmful eating habits and conduct yourself in a

healthful manner. Eat only when you are hungry and drink only when thirsty.
2) Do not eat until your stomach is filled, but only eat to three-quarters satiation. Don't drink water during the meal. Drink only after the food begins to digest. Do some light exercise, such as walking, before the meal.
3) A day is 24 hours long. Sleep eight hours.
4) Don't sleep immediately after a meal; instead, wait three to four hours after eating.
5) Food that is easily digestible such as grapes, berries, and melons should be eaten at the beginning of the meal and should not be mixed with other foods.
6) When eating poultry and beef in one meal, eat the poultry first. The same applies to eggs and beef: eat the eggs first. A general rule is always to eat the light food first.
7) Another general rule regarding the body's health is that one who engages in rigorous exercise and does not eat to satiation will avoid sickness and be strengthened, even if he eats unhealthy foods.
8) Conversely, one who is inactive, even if he eats healthy foods, will suffer pain and a weakening of the body.
9) In general, overeating – even healthful foods – is poisonous to the body and is the source of most illnesses.
10) And as King Solomon said: "One who guards his mouth and tongue, protects himself from harm"; that is, guard your mouth from unhealthy foods and overeating, and your tongue from excessive speech.

10 principles of successful investing

Just as Maimonides provided a sound plan for healthy eating, successful financial analysts have developed a plan for healthy investing.

But unlike Maimonides, financial planners cannot guarantee results. In fact, with the exception of some insurance-related products, promising guaranteed results is prohibited by government regulations that oversee the conduct of investment advisors. Indeed, investment products' performance reports usually have a tag line warning the reader that "past performance is no guarantee of future results."

In my opinion, however, the following "10 Principles of Successful Investing" offers investors the greatest likelihood of financial success:

1) Self-discipline, not income level, determines your ability to save money.
2) If your "safe" investments don't outpace inflation, your investments are not truly safe as there is potential for decreased purchasing power due to inflation risk.
3) Don't try to "time"[1] the stock market; those who do so usually fail.
4) Your investments should be part of an overall strategy designed to pursue your specific financial objectives.
5) Substantial growth of assets over a long term requires some equity investments, which can be volatile. The percentage of equities in your portfolio should be compatible with your tolerance for risk.

---

1. "Timing" the market refers to the attempt by investors to predict when to invest or sell. They hope to buy low and sell high.

6) The most efficient portfolios are properly diversified,[2] both within and among the basic asset categories.[3]
7) The most successful investors are patient, long-term investors.
8) Investing should be as systematic as paying your monthly bills.[4]
9) You should take a holistic approach to your financial life, recognizing that tax strategies, insurance needs and investment goals are interrelated.
10) You should find a knowledgeable tax and financial advisor you can trust.

---

2. Diversification does not assure or guarantee better performance and cannot eliminate the risk of investment losses.
3. The two most common broad asset classes are equities (stocks) and fixed income securities (bonds). A diversified portfolio first determines the allocation between these two asset classes. Each of these classes can be further diversified. Bonds include U.S. Treasury bonds, corporate bonds and others. Equities include large and small corporations (via the stock market) as well as international entities and real estate.
4. Periodic investment plans do not assure a profit against loss in declining markets. Such plans involve continuous investment in securities regardless of fluctuating price levels of such securities. An investor should consider his or her financial ability to continue his or her purchases through periods of low price levels.

Chapter 1

AN INTRODUCTION TO INVESTING

AMERICA'S WEALTH

The American (United States) economy was and continues to be the greatest wealth generator in history. To benefit from this economic miracle, you do not have to be a financial wizard or a great risk taker. You just have to believe in the capitalist free-market system and choose to participate.

Just how enormous has this wealth generator been?

To illustrate, let's look at a real-life example. The first mutual fund in America is the Massachusetts Investor Trust (MITTX). It was started in 1924 by a company now known as MFS Investment Management. The investment objective of the fund[1] is to seek capital appreciation appropriate for long-term investors who do not require current income.

Had you invested $25 per month in the Massachusetts Investor Trust from the fund's inception on July 15, 1924 through March 31, 2015, your entire investment over the period would have been $27,225. The *value* of your investment on March 31, 2015, with dividends reinvested, would be $12,612,852.[2]

Here are two additional examples of wealth created by "average" people:

---

1. Prospectus dated April 30, 2014.
2. This information was provided by MFS Funds as prepared by Morningstar on June 11, 2015. Past performance does not guarantee future results; that the investment return and principal value of an investment will fluctuate so that an investor's shares, when redeemed, may be worth more or less than their original cost; and that current performance may be lower or higher than the performance data quoted. The performance of the fund for quarter ended 3/31/2015 was 1.25, 1 year 10.82, 5 years 13.07, 10 years 8.49. Gross expense ratio is 0.78.

Evanston woman leaves $18 million to hospital

Chicago Sun-Times, July 31, 1997 – A retired secretary from Evanston, known as the "Teddy Bear Lady," bequeathed an $18 million fortune to Children's Memorial Hospital for medical research. Gladys Holm made her fortune investing savings from her salary, which hit an estimated high of $15,000 a year before she retired in 1969. She died in 1996 at age 86. Few friends suspected that Holm, who lived in a modest two-bedroom apartment, was wealthy.

Gladys' boss advised her to invest her yearly bonus in the stock market, a long-time friend said. "If he bought 1,000 shares of some company, Gladys would buy 10 shares of the same thing. Nobody gave her that money; she earned it."

STAGGERING BEQUESTS BY UNASSUMING COUPLE

Brooklyn couple leaves estate valued at $800 million

The New York Times, July 13, 1998 – Professor Donald Othmer and his wife Mildred lived modestly. They had a townhouse in Brooklyn. They rode the subway. And when they decided to invest, they entrusted their money to an old friend from Nebraska. Their friend was Warren Buffett, and in the 1960s, they each invested $25,000 in his investment partnership. In the early 1970s they received shares in Berkshire Hathaway, then valued at $42 a share.

When the Othmers died at ages 90 and 91, their stock was worth $77,200 a share, leaving a whopping estate worth an estimated $800 million.

Regrettably, too many people have *not* participated in this economic phenomenon. Wondering why this is so, I recalled my family's own investment experience. My family immigrated to the United States in 1964 and within days, my father began working as a mechanic. A few months later, relatives who lived here longer and were "experienced" in investments, introduced my parents to the stock market by recommending a stock. My parents bought 100 shares of the stock for a total of $725. When the value of the stock declined to $340 a few days later, my parents sold the stock and forever swore they'd never invest in the market again. And they never did. All their savings were "invested" in the bank where it was "safe" (and never grew very much).

A more recent example of why people might be afraid to invest involves some unfortunate investors and an unscrupulous, amateur investment advisor who preyed on their ignorance:

A few years ago, I was asked to assist in establishing a pension plan for the teachers at a local private school. At a meeting with the teachers, I explained to them the importance of providing for their retirement. In addition, I stressed the importance of staying with their investment strategy as there would be times when the stock market would decline and the value of the pension would fall.

The pension plan was established and teachers began to make monthly contributions to their account. Then a wonderful thing happened, but, through no fault of their own, the teachers thought it was a disaster. The year was 2001 and the stock market declined sharply and continued to decline in 2002. The funds in which they were invested had a 12% decline in the first year and an additional 16% the following year.

I received frantic calls from some nervous teachers and even from some of their spouses. "Do something!" they pleaded with me. "We can't afford to lose our money. This is all we've got." It is emotionally painful to listen to such calls, but I asked them to be patient and stick with the plan. The most important thing to remember, I explained, is that as investors, they are buyers of shares in mutual funds. I told them to "consider the decline as a sale. If cans of tuna were sold at 25% below regular prices, wouldn't you rush to buy them? Stock market declines are natural. If you want to participate and make money in the stock market, you must be willing to tolerate the declines." Unfortunately, without proper guidance, fear almost always dominates logic.

One of the teachers contacted a newly minted investment advisor who was really an insurance agent. At a hastily arranged meeting, he warned the teachers that it was possible for them to lose their entire investment and that he had an alternative investment that was guaranteed not to lose any money. A panicked person will almost always choose safety, and he was throwing them a lifeline. They all switched to the high-priced (high-commission) annuity he recommended. He was right. They would not lose any money, but they would not make any, either.

In the three years after they began investing with the new advisor, their portfolio had averaged a return of 3% per year. During the same three-year period, the stock market represented by the S&P 500 returned 28.36%, 10.74% and 4.83%.[3]

Indeed, the American economy has been the healthiest generator of wealth in the world. Those who weathered the ups and downs of their various investments reaped the benefits. Those who were motivated by fear and panicked, often lost.

---

3. http://www.stern.nyu.edu/~adamodar/pc/datasets/histretSP.html

The cliché in the gym is "no pain, no gain." If you want to reap the great rewards of investing in the market, you'll have to accept the "pain" of temporary declines.

The rest of this book will provide valuable information and guidance on how to invest wisely.

INVESTMENT GLOSSARY

Before we continue, here is a short list of investment terminology as well as some behavioral terms that may reflect the investor's varied emotional states during the investing process.

Greed: A selfish desire to have more of something (especially money).

Fear: An expectation or worry about something bad or unpleasant.

Irrational: Not thinking clearly; not able to use reason or good judgment.

In the short term, the financial markets are driven by greed and irrational fear.

To invest successfully, one should:

> "...simply attempt to be fearful when others are greedy, and to be greedy only when others are fearful." – Warren Buffett[4]
>
> "A lot of people with high IQs are terrible investors because they've got terrible temperaments. That is why we say that having a certain kind of temperament is more important than brains. You need to keep raw, irrational emotion under control." – Charles Munger

---

4. Author's note: To invest successfully, one should not follow the crowds; rather, one should be a contrarian and avoid the "herd" mentality.

The following are explanations of terms that will be helpful as you read further.

Short-Term Investing: Investments that are bought and sold in less than three years.

Long-Term Investing: Investments that one keeps for more than five years.

Over the short term, the financial markets are volatile. Cash needed for the short term should be kept in a bank's money market accounts, Certificates of Deposit (CDs) or very short-term U.S. Government Treasury bonds. However, for long-term investments, two quotes from Warren Buffett, the most successful investor of the 20th century, are worth heeding:

> "Over the long term, the stock market news will be good."
>
> "In the 20th century, the United States endured two World Wars and other traumatic and expensive military conflicts: the Depression; a dozen or so recessions and financial panics; oil shocks; a flu epidemic; and the resignation of a disgraced president. Yet the Dow Jones Industrial Average (rose from 66 to 11,497)."[5]

Bond: A legal contract in which the government or a company promises to pay back an amount of money that it borrowed, along with interest earned on that borrowed money.

Stock: A share of the value of a company which can be bought, sold, or traded as an investment.

---

5. The Dow Jones Industrial Average (DJIA) is a price-weighted average of 30 significant stocks traded on the New York Stock Exchange and the NASDAQ (National Association of Securities Dealers Automated Quotations). At the time of the writing of this book, the Dow was over 18,000.

Stock Market: The market in which shares of publicly held companies are issued and traded either through exchanges or over-the-counter markets.

> People ask, "Isn't the stock market risky?"
>
> The stock market is simply a place to trade stocks. The question should be: "Are stocks, which constitute the ownership of companies, risky?" Some companies fail; many don't. The Standard and Poor's 500 (S&P 500) index includes 500 of the United States' large cap corporations.[6] From the moment you wake up and throughout the day, you encounter hundreds of products produced by these companies: soap, toothpaste, towels, cereal, milk, coffee, cars, gasoline, newspapers, telephones, electricity, medicines, computers, entertainment, restaurants, etc... real companies making valuable products. Modern society cannot exist without these products.
>
> With a single investment in a mutual fund or an ETF that tracks the S&P 500 index, you can own a share in these 500 companies.

Mutual Fund: A professionally managed pool of funds collected from many investors for the purpose of investing in securities such as stocks and bonds. A mutual fund's portfolio is structured and maintained to match the investment objectives stated in its prospectus. The main advantage of mutual funds is that they give investors access to professionally managed, diversified portfolios of equities, bonds and other securities.

Some of the disadvantages of mutual funds include high expense ratios and possible sales charges, tax inefficiencies, and possible excessive trading by the fund's manager. The fund's prospectus contains the facts that an investor needs

---

6. See first entry in Appendix C, p. 161, for definition.

to make an informed investment decision and should be read prior to investing in mutual funds.

> The choice for long-term investors is to be a business owner (via stocks) or a creditor (via bonds). With stock ownership, investors share in the success or failure of the company, while the creditor who invests in bonds receives a fixed income.
>
> Ownership of a business generally results in greater reward to the owners than to the creditors, but an owner shoulders a greater risk. To help reduce the risk, investment in a mutual fund offers diversification, thereby reducing the risk of owning a limited number of companies.[7]

Volatility: A change – either up or down, and sometimes dramatically – in the price of an investment, regardless of whether it is a bond, stock, mutual fund, real estate or other types of investments over a short time period.

Market Correction: A decline of at least 10% in the value of a stock, bond or index such as the S&P 500 or DJIA. In general, corrections have historically been a temporary price decline, interrupting an uptrend in the market value of an asset or index.

> A market correction is an opportunity for the patient, long-term investor. When prices decline during a correction, a long-term investor may have the opportunity to purchase shares of companies at a discounted price.

Bull Market: A period of generally rising stock prices, characterized by optimism and investor confidence. It is a time when the stock market appears to be in a long-term climb and investors

---

7. Please note: Diversification does not assure or guarantee better performance and cannot eliminate the risk of investment losses.

are more likely to buy stocks. The optimism often leads to euphoria and investors become less cautious in their investment strategies.

Bear Market: A market condition in which prices of securities are falling due to widespread pessimism. It generally entails a decline of 20% or more in broad market indexes, such as the Dow Jones Industrial Average (DJIA) or the Standard & Poor's 500 Index, over at least a two-month period.

> *"You make most of your money in a bear market — you just don't realize it at the time."*
> – Shelby Cullom Davis
>
> *"Bear markets are when stocks return to their rightful ownership."*[8]
> – Nick Murray

"This time it's different": A frequently used excuse to avoid or delay investing.

> *"There are always things to worry about and hundreds of reasons not to invest. Those who abandon stocks because of fear and uncertainty may pay a tremendous price. History has shown that a diversified portfolio of equities held for the long term has been the best way to build real wealth."*
> – Shelby Cullom Davis

---

8. Author's note: In the Talmud (*Arachin* 23a), Abaye commented that "Poverty follows after the poor." Poor people seem to have circumstances that conspire against them which prevent them from bettering their state. During bear markets, people panic and sell their investments at a low price, while the wealthy follow their advisor's advice and buy.

Simplicity Is the Ultimate Sophistication
"The Rest Is Commentary"

Rabbi (Reb) Hillel, one of the most influential sages of the first century BCE, was known for his kindness, gentleness, and wisdom. One of his most famous sayings, recorded in the book *Ethics of Our Fathers*, is: "If I am not for myself, who will be? And if I am only for myself, what am I? And if not now, when?"

A contemporary of Reb Hillel was the great sage Reb Shammai, known for his quick temper and strict interpretation of the Torah (the Jewish Bible). A gentile seeking to convert to Judaism once approached Reb Shammai and demanded to be taught the whole Torah quickly "while standing on one foot." Reb Shammai refused the foolhardy request and drove the man out of his presence. When the man approached Reb Hillel with the same impudent demand, Hillel accepted him, saying:

> *"That which is hateful to you, do not do unto another: This is the whole Torah. The rest is commentary."*

The Bible contains an infinite body of knowledge that was interpreted by the *Mishnah*, Talmud, and thousands of books authored by Torah scholars, yet according to Hillel, it can all be condensed into a simple statement.

Obviously, Hillel was not implying that we should abandon learning the Bible and seeking its deeper meaning. As a leading Torah scholar, he served as the president of the Sanhedrin, the supreme court of Jewish law, with a mission to strengthen Torah knowledge and observance among the Jewish people.

Hillel, in fact, endured great self-sacrifice for the sake of Torah study. A poor woodcutter, the Babylonian-born Hillel migrated to Israel in order to learn the teachings of the Torah. He endured such dire poverty that he was unable to pay the entrance fee to the Torah study hall. It is said that he climbed up to the roof of the study hall to eavesdrop through the chimney. On a particularly cold winter evening, he nearly froze to death on the roof, straining to hear what was being taught in the warm study hall below.

Upon seeing Hillel's exemplary drive to learn the Torah at all costs, the Sages abolished these admission fees – a ruling which applies until today. Torah learning is greatly encouraged; however, as we delve into the sea of Torah knowledge, we must remember the singular underlying purpose of our learning, as Hillel did. Although he was an extremely learned person who devoted his life to Torah learning, the core of his learning revolved around the "simple" phrase he told the gentile.

Similarly, scientists are constantly searching for the unifying principle that will explain the universe. Einstein's Theory of Relativity, $E=mc^2$, is just that: a "simple" formula that reduces the laws of the universe to the simplest and most elegant form. To quote Einstein:

> *"Make everything as simple as possible, but not simpler."*

When it comes to my investment philosophy, I follow the same principle. In my more than forty years of work as a Certified Public Accountant and advisor, and having dealt with numerous clients and observed the financial lives and investment habits of people, I believe that financial success, too, has one single, most important, concept:

Successful investing should be simple and boring.

"Simple" does not mean unsophisticated, as Leonardo da Vinci once said: "Simplicity is the ultimate sophistication."

And why should it be "boring"? Because successful investing should have a long-term focus. Often, doing nothing is the best "course of action." It can prevent you from making investment mistakes.

After these two rules of thumb, the rest is financial commentary, which will be explained in the remainder of this book.

It is unfortunate that people believe that the more complicated and "sophisticated" an investment program is, the better their returns will be. How else was Madoff able to attract billions of investors' dollars?

Hedge funds, which are typically available to "sophisticated" investors who have at least one million dollars to invest, are another unfortunate example of a complex but poor investment, in my opinion. In his book *The Hedge Fund Mirage*, Simon Lack writes, "If all the money that has ever been invested in hedge funds had been put into Treasury Bills instead, the results would have been twice as good."

Perhaps that's why the California Public Employee's Retirement System (CalPERS), which manages almost $300 billion in assets, announced that it was divesting of all of the hedge funds in its portfolio. You can learn a lot by CalPERS decision to dump hedge funds.

A "simple" investment does not mean that it is made ignorantly. Gaining knowledge and understanding of your finances will greatly increase your chance of success, but so will recognizing your limitations.

For many people, boredom can arouse one's desire to take action because as the saying goes, "Doing nothing feels foolish," and excitement pretends to be boredom's cure. This is especially so in light of the daily hyped-up media reports of the latest recommendations by experts who, incidentally, often contradict one another! Regrettably, excitement is the nemesis of investing success.

In every investment decision you make, ask yourself whether you are making this investment only for the sake of doing something. In my experience, once an investment strategy is in place, doing nothing – that is, not deviating from your strategy – is generally the best course of action.

Another pitfall is listening to the media. CNBC, Bloomberg, or Fox Business News will often display a second-by-second countdown to a financial announcement on the bottom of the TV screen. The excitement builds and it incites investors to take action. I know this first-hand, as clients often call my office asking what action I am taking in anticipation of a certain event. My first response is to remind them of the previous time they called me in the same state of excitement, and how taking no action at that time proved to be the correct decision.

I also remind them that the media's first and foremost objective is to provide entertainment. Investing is a serious matter and should be approached in a thoughtful manner, not reduced to thoughtless entertainment or fabricated excitement. What it *does* do is increase the media's viewer or listener-ship which ultimately augments its *own* revenue. This "financial entertainment" does not contribute to your financial success; in fact, it hinders it.

Bob Arnott, founder and chairman of Research Affiliates, is quoted as saying, "Successful investing is not difficult; it is just painful" – and the emotional pain is triggered by our ups and downs on the rollercoaster of fear and greed. We feel calm and confident when the markets are up, and we become fearful when the markets are down. During a market downturn, we are fearful of losing all our money. The future looks bleak – even though in the long-run it is not – and we are quick to panic and sell. When the markets are up, hearing about the great success stories of those who cashed in prompts us to invest.

The solution is to develop a strategic investment plan based on your goals; goals that you understand. Unless your goals change, the most prudent thing you can do is to adhere to that plan.

Successful investing should be "simple." The rest is commentary.

Profoundly "simple" advice

At a private meeting with the Lubavitcher Rebbe, a man asked the Rebbe for advice regarding his *sholom bayis* (marital) issues. "My wife is on the verge of a nervous breakdown. We have five children and the oldest is six years old; my wife is extremely stressed and always irritable. It is affecting our relationship. I thought that perhaps I should buy her a piece of jewelry, or maybe we should dine out once in a while. I am asking the Rebbe for advice on how to deal with the situation."

Following a short pause, the Rebbe addressed the husband, saying, "I am not sure if your suggestions will work, but I am sure that if you wash the dishes after dinner, that will definitely help."

THE FOUNDATION FOR SUCCESSFUL LIVING

Marriage and finance

Honoring one's wife:

> *A man must always be careful about his wife's honor, because blessing is found in a person's house only in the merit of his wife....*
>
> *This is what Rava said: "Honor your wife in order that you may become wealthy."* — Talmud, Bava Metzia 59a

Develop a strategy and stick with it:
Comparing marriage and investment strategies

I am not a very adventurous person, nor one who runs after the latest fads. Perhaps my life as a Torah-observant Jew helped me formulate my life's attitude: to search for the truth, and when I find it, embrace it and commit myself to it.

My daily life revolves around well-established routines that subsume my entire being. I am committed to this way of life and find comfort in it. Commitments and routines (habits) simplify life and enable one to live a more successful and less stressful life.

For example, marriage should be based on shared values and the husband's and wife's commitment to each other. Recent studies[9] claim that romance decreases over time and eventually ends. Without shared values, what is left? Presumably, love based on romance will go the way of the romance, whereas love based on mutual respect and shared values can only continue to grow (and maintain the romance).

---
9. "A Phenomenological Study of Falling Out of Love," Joanni L. Sailor, Cameron University, Lawton, Oklahoma, USA.

In my community, we believe in marrying early and raising a family as soon as possible. Girls generally get married at around twenty; the boys around twenty-two. There is no reason to wait until they are older. Once they meet someone who shares their values and goals and they are attracted to each other, the young people marry. The courtship usually takes from two to four weeks, followed by the wedding within two to three months.

Chani, my son Moshe's future bride, was mentioned to us through a matchmaker. We "investigated" her by contacting her teachers and mutual friends of our two families. Likewise, her family "investigated" Moshe. Once the inquiries indicated that the prospective bride was suitable for my son, and her parents approved Moshe as a prospective groom, a date was arranged. They met on a Saturday evening and discussed their interests and goals. They were sufficiently attracted to each other, and by their own choice they agreed to meet again two days later on Monday night.

At the end of their third date on Wednesday night, they decided to get engaged, and a few weeks later they were married.

When I relate my son's experience to others, they are skeptical. "How can two people get engaged after only three dates?" "Do they love each other?" But at this point in the budding relationship, what does love have to do with it? You may have heard the song *Do You Love Me?* from *Fiddler on the Roof*. I believe that love is a very serious and beautiful thing that develops *after* one has married.

From our vantage point as parents, we found out as much as we could about Chani and found her qualities and outlook on life to be a perfect fit for Moshe. We were obviously uncertain about their love at such an early stage but hoped that with shared values, goals, and a commitment to make the marriage succeed, it would come.

The matchmaking process beautifully parallels my investment philosophy:

INVESTMENT	MARRIAGE
Investigate	Investigate
Set goals and expectations	Common goals and values
Be comfortable with your strategy	Be comfortable with your spouse
Commitment to strategy	Commitment to family
Avoid the latest fads	Do not look elsewhere
Roadmap to success	Low divorce rate

Incidentally, the divorce rate in our community is very low, and couples are generally satisfied with their marriages. This is in contrast to the general populace where people never stop wondering if somebody out there is better for them, and singles constantly ask themselves, "Should I put off making a commitment? Should I look around a little more?" Without finding, or even looking for, someone with shared core values, they continue to look further and further but never seem to be satisfied. When this mindset affects married couples, one can speculate that perhaps this is why the divorce rate is so high.

Chapter 2

THE IMPORTANCE OF A FINANCIAL COACH

ALL YOU NEED IS INFORMATION... REALLY?

Two days after leaving his small village, the poor and simple peasant finally arrived at his cousin's great mansion in the big city. His cousin was one of the richest men in the city and was well known for his philanthropy. The poor cousin was in dire financial straits and was visiting in the hope that his wealthy cousin would help him.

After gathering his courage, he rang the bell and identified himself to the gatekeeper. His cousin warmly greeted him and invited him to stay in the beautiful mansion with him.

In honor of the guest, a great feast was prepared. After the family and the guest were seated around the large dining room table, the poor peasant observed to his surprise that no food was served. However, following a bit of chatting, the wealthy host reached for a small copper bell and, at the sound of the bell's ringing, four waiters suddenly appeared with trays laden with gourmet appetizers for the first course. The poor cousin could not believe his eyes.

A while later, following a ring of the bell, the waiters reappeared to remove the dishes. Another ring of the bell brought the second course. And so it continued throughout the seven-course meal, during which the poor cousin stared at the bell, pondering its wondrous properties.

On the second day of his visit, the poor peasant felt it was time to approach his cousin and describe his problems to him.

"My dear cousin," said the wealthy one, "of course I am willing to help you. Just tell me what you need."

The poor cousin was ready with his request. "May I please have the bell?" he stammered.

"The bell?" the wealthy cousin asked. "Why would you want the bell? I am willing to give you as much money as you need."

"He is only willing to give me money because the bell is more valuable," the peasant thought to himself, and again requested the bell. The wealthy cousin was surprised at the strange request, but without hesitation gave the bell to his poor cousin. The peasant was thrilled.

Immediately upon his return home, the peasant gathered his family and friends to his humble cottage and announced that they should prepare for a feast. They looked curiously at each other, and then at the poor peasant, since they could not imagine enjoying a feast in this shack. Noticing the curious glances and whispers, he told them about the miraculous bell his cousin had given him. As they were all seated around the table, he unwrapped the bell carefully and with great vigor began to ring it.

Nothing happened.

"Maybe I rang the bell the wrong way," he thought. He tried to remember the exact hand motion his cousin used. Still there were no results. No waiters and no food appeared. As the crowd around the table began to mock and jeer him, the peasant angrily announced that his cousin had tricked him: He had switched the bells!

Does information equal wisdom?

> "The only source of knowledge is experience."
> —Albert Einstein

In the analogy of the peasant, his wealthy cousin, and the bell, the peasant naively attributed the origin of the cousin's wealth to the ringing of a bell. Sometimes, in our lives, we think that "ringing a bell" will bring us what we desire, but we soon find out that the "bell" is just the end product of hard work, experience and knowledge.

The internet has revolutionized personal finance and investments. We live today in an information age, and the whole world seems to be in a hurry. Regarding investing in the stock market, one commentator said, "Every second counts." Another encourages us to make money decisions *here and now, every day,* insisting that we must make quick decisions. What is important to understand, however, is that we suffer from information overload. There is simply too much information available.

If you log onto the Google search engine and type in the word "money," you will get a choice of over 2.5 billion possible websites. If you type in the word "invest," you will get "only" around 277 million possible websites.

How long will it take for you to sift through all that information? How much do you really need? You have access to all the information you could ever want at your fingertips, but does that make your life easier? Does it make you smarter? What is the value of such a huge quantity of information?

In reality, the challenge is not to acquire or access the information. The challenge is to distill the important facts from the many sources that are available today. Are we able to sort it out and use it wisely?

The period 1995-2000 began with a bull market,[1] but soon the euphoria over the growth potential of the internet developed into an irrational speculative bubble that became known as the *"dot com bubble."* The value of equity markets led by the technology-dominated NASDAQ index rose rapidly from under 1,000 to a peak of 5,132.52 on March 10, 2000.[2]

---

1. See the chapter entitled "Investment Glossary" for a definition of "bull market."
2. Wikipedia, "Dot-com boom and bust."

Equity values in the internet sector and related fields were rising rapidly, and all one needed to do was buy any internet/technology focused mutual fund or technology/internet stock in order to make money. But when the market collapsed in 2000-2001, people incurred substantial losses. Although plenty of information was available warning that the stocks were extremely overpriced, many filtered out what they wanted to ignore and listened only to what they wished to hear.

"Two things drive the market: greed and fear." Even if we have said these words before, they bear repeating, and they are worthy of memorizing. Two things drive the market: greed and fear.

Today, people are still as greedy as ever when the market rises, and just as fearful and nervous when it falls. The difference is that now, because they have more information than ever at their fingertips, they make the same mistakes more quickly. Financial advisors refer to the financial news media as "financial pornography" because it caters to people's baser needs. First, when the market looks hopeful, the news stokes their greedy desire to make a great deal of money quickly. Then, when the market turns downward, the media instills fear in people so as to encourage them to abandon their investment strategy.

Don't ask for the bell when what you really want is the dinner

A visit to the financial section of a local bookstore may impress you and even convince you that there is an easy way to become financially successful. Warren Buffett is without question the most successful investor of our time — which you will quickly find out when you pick up one of the dozens of books about him, with such titles as *The Buffett Way* and *How to Pick Stocks Like Warren Buffett*. Read a few of these books, or any of the other compelling titles on the bookshelves, and you may believe you are on your way to vast wealth.

But are these books similar to the infamous "bell"? I'm afraid they are. Can the wisdom, experience, and temperament of a successful investor be transmitted in a book? Can you possibly imitate Warren Buffett by simply "ringing a bell" or reading a book about his investment strategy? I believe not. Just as you would never make a serious medical decision without personally consulting a doctor, decisions regarding your personal, highly individual financial future should be made in consultation with financial professionals.

If you are still considering the do-it-yourself method, ask yourself a question:

How much time are you willing to devote to obtain the skills and knowledge necessary to invest successfully? Investing is difficult, time-consuming and emotionally taxing, and while some skills may be learned, it is necessary to keep a well-known quote from Warren Buffett in mind:

> Most people get interested in stocks when everyone else is. [However], the time to get interested is when no one else is. You cannot buy what is popular and do well.

Our natural dispositions are our worst enemy when it comes to investing. (See chart below on the Emotional Cycle of Investing, p. 29.) While we may be able to develop an efficient portfolio that matches our risk profile – a portfolio that is properly diversified and tax-efficient – do we have the ability to hang in there when the market declines? Can you be greedy when everyone is fearful and fearful when everyone is greedy (another of Buffett's quotes)? Investors know that they should buy low and sell high, but when the markets experience a downturn, fear sets in and they are quick to sell.

Dalbar's Quantitative Analysis of Investor Behavior

Since 1994, Dalbar's Quantitative Analysis of Investor Behavior (QAIB) has been measuring the effects of investor decisions to buy, sell and switch into and out of mutual funds over both short and long-term time frames. The results consistently show that investors make poor investment choices, driven often by emotions, and on average earn less – in many cases, much less – than mutual fund performance reports would suggest.

Dalbar annually updates its QAIB study, which shows how the average equity fund investor performed over various time periods in comparison to the markets. The findings are consistent over the years: The results show that the average investor in mutual funds earns less than the mutual fund performances themselves because the investors don't stay in it for the long-term. For example, for the period 1994-2013, the S&P 500 returned an annualized 9.22% while the average mutual fund investor earned about 5.02% per year.[3]

Similar results apply to fixed-income investors. During the same twenty-year period, average fixed-income investors' returns were 0.71% while the Barclay Aggregate Bond index returned 5.74%.[4]

---

3. QAIB 2014.
4. *Ibid.*

The Cycle of Investor Emotions

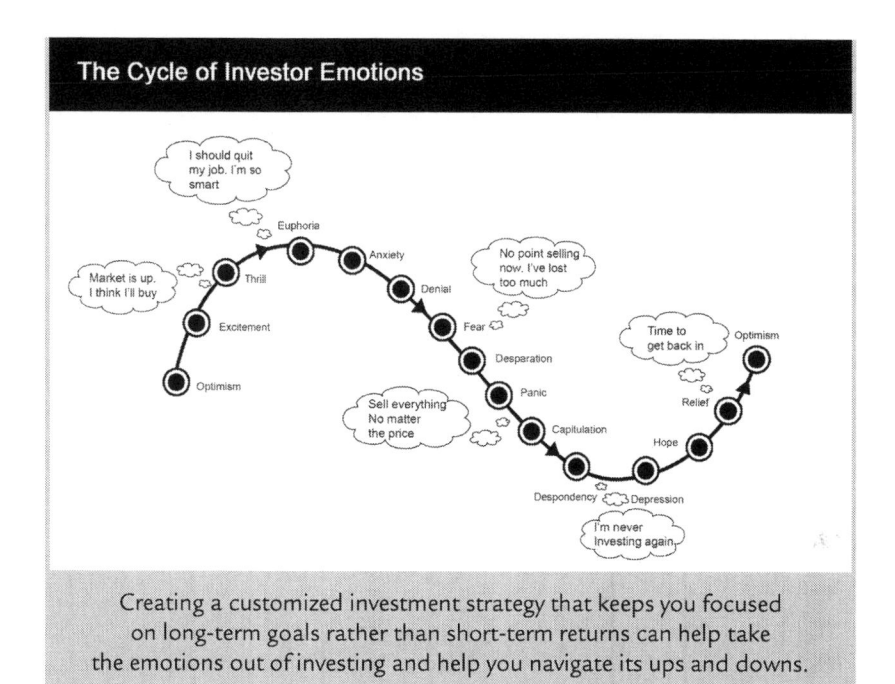

- Optimism
- Market is up. I think I'll buy
- Thrill
- Excitement
- Euphoria — I should quit my job. I'm so smart
- Anxiety
- Denial — No point selling now. I've lost too much
- Fear
- Desperation
- Panic — Sell everything No matter the price
- Capitulation
- Despondency
- Depression — I'm never investing again
- Hope
- Relief
- Optimism
- Time to get back in

Creating a customized investment strategy that keeps you focused on long-term goals rather than short-term returns can help take the emotions out of investing and help you navigate its ups and downs.

Another question: If you were a stranger, would you hire someone with *your* qualifications to manage your serious money? In selecting an individual to manage your money, I believe you would never dream of hiring a person who:

1) Is not licensed.
2) Lacks investment experience.
3) Has limited knowledge of income taxes, which are the consequences of investment decisions.
4) Has no client besides you.
5) Has limited time to continuously monitor your portfolio.
6) Lacks the tools available to professional financial advisors.

Acknowledging a layman's limitations is just one more reason why consulting a financial professional is essential for managing your serious money: money that will fund your children's education, your retirement, or other important goals. If you wish to experience some excitement and feel that trading stocks will feed that urge, set aside a small percentage of your portfolio for that purpose.

I think the point is clear. When it comes to investing your money, you would do well to speak to a financial advisor and make use of his or her education and experience. When such a person has lived through a variety of financial time periods – both bull and bear markets – and has successfully advised numerous clients over the course of his career, it would be wise to choose the seasoned professional and leave the bell with the wealthy cousin.

A Financial Advisor

> *Without strategies, a nation will fall, but salvation lies in much counsel.* (Just as a nation must use every available means to overcome attack, so too must an individual seek advice in facing his battles.)   *Mishlei (Proverbs)* 11:14

The poor peasant was at his wits' end. After struggling for so many years, he only had a few hundred shekels to his name. Now his oldest daughter was getting married and he had to come up with a hefty sum to cover his share of the wedding costs.

"I have to pay for the food," he said, rubbing his forehead.

"And the violin players," he said, rubbing it again.

"And the wedding gown!" At that, he smacked his head so hard, he fell backwards. And when he stood up, he smacked it again. "All this will cost me at least 10,000 shekels!" he cried. "I don't even own a sack that big — let alone the money to fill it!"

In his desperation and not knowing which way to turn, he put his faith in G-d.

He reached for a pen and paper and wrote a letter to G-d, listing all his requirements for the wedding. "This is what I need, G-d," he wrote, and sealed the letter. With that, he went to the front of his ramshackle house, waited for the postman, and handed him the letter.

Then he waited for an answer.

When the post office clerk received the strange envelope addressed to G-d, he decided to direct it to the richest man in town – who everyone thought was next to G-d anyway since he had so much money.

Thus the postman delivered the letter to the rich man who was deeply moved by the outpouring of the peasant's heart.

"This," he said, "is a good man who deserves my help."

So he decided to send the peasant 5,000 shekels, half the amount requested.

"What a miracle!" cried the peasant when he received the money, raising his arms aloft. "Thank you, G-d."

And with that money and the money he was able to raise from others, he made his daughter's wedding.

Two years later, the peasant needed to marry off his second daughter. So he wrote another letter to G-d, and again, the postman delivered it to the richest man in town.

"That ungrateful man!" exclaimed the rich man. "He is asking me for money again when he never even had the decency to thank me for what I gave him the first time!"

It was as he was about to shred the letter that he noticed the postscript at the bottom of the page: "P.S. G-d, this time, please **do not** *send the money through the rich man. He has plenty, but he still kept half for himself."*

Accepting professional guidance

What should your expectations be when beseeching assistance, as in the above story, or when retaining a professional advisor? The following chapters review the role of an advisor. But the ultimate responsibility for the success of a program is with the client: initially in selecting the appropriate advisor and then following through with his or her recommendations.

"Obese."

The word jumped out at me as I looked over the nurse's shoulder at my chart on the computer. I knew I was 35 pounds overweight, but was that all it took to be considered obese? To augment my surprise, I saw that my cholesterol levels were high and I was diagnosed as being "pre-diabetic."

These were the results of my annual physical examination. I was directed to see a nutritionist, Ms. Levine. In the past I had successfully followed a number of diets on my own, including Fit for Life, Atkins, South Beach Diet, and Accu-Weight Weight Loss, among others. I was successful with those diets – that is, until I failed and regained all my weight.

Now that the situation was serious, I needed professional guidance. Meeting with Ms. Levine proved invaluable. The first meeting was a discovery meeting, and following a lecture about the consequences of continuing my current eating habits, we formulated an eating plan. We continued to meet monthly and then, as I was showing success in following her guidance, we met quarterly. A follow-up blood test revealed that my cholesterol level had dropped by about 18% and I had reached my goal weight.

I have kept the weight off for over a year now and I am confident that with my new eating habits and the nutritionist's continual monitoring, it will stay off.

Why was I successful this time?

The Torah relates the story of Joseph, whose brothers sold him into slavery. He ended up in Egypt as a slave to Potiphar, a high-ranking minister in Pharaoh's court.

Joseph was a good-looking young man. On numerous occasions, Potiphar's wife attempted to seduce him, but he refused her advances. Finally, one day when the two were alone in her home, she was more forceful in her efforts. Joseph nearly succumbed to her advances, but at the last moment he escaped. Our Sages explain that at that moment, he saw a vision of his holy father, Jacob, and was unable to commit such a serious transgression.

On numerous occasions, I was also tempted to "transgress" my food plan. It was the vision of a disapproving look from Ms. Levine and her words that kept me in line.

Now I don't think one has to fear one's nutritionist (or one's financial advisor) to gain benefit from their wisdom, but advice coming from a professional surely has its merits!

What is the role of a financial advisor?

In his fitness book *Body for Life*, Bill Phillips promises to be the success coach who will help you discover your true potential, helping you stay on track and avoid setbacks. He describes his regimen and, to motivate his readers, asks, "Could you have done more if I were standing right there, encouraging you to reach ever higher – to push yourself further?"

Financial planning is a serious matter, and your financial well-being works in a similar way. An investment portfolio can be compared to a symphony orchestra. Just as a symphony needs a conductor, a healthy, harmonious financial life needs a personal financial conductor. The amount of information on the various products available today is mind-numbing. Information overload does not lead to smart choices; on the contrary, it leads to paralysis or ill-advised decisions.

It is my belief that a financial advisor should be contacted before making an investment or committing money to a business transaction.

An offer from the bank officer: two tales

David and Anne came to my office to review an investment that their local bank's investment advisor had offered them. They were excited about it. In an environment of 1.5% CDs, the investment advisor had offered them a 4.75% CD for five years, with the flexibility to withdraw their money whenever they chose.

They would have made the investment immediately had they not remembered my cautioning them to contact me *before* committing themselves to any financial transaction. When I asked for a document describing the offer, they stated simply that it was a verbal offer from the bank officer and they were sure it was legitimate.

Knowing that the product they described is unavailable, I asked them to return to the bank and ask for a prospectus (a legal document that provides details about an investment offering). I explained that the investment was probably a fixed annuity with withdrawal surrender charges and a lower interest rate than they were quoted. They doubted my opinion – after all, "a bank made the offer" – but promised to return the following day with the prospectus.

They returned the next day and told me that just as I suspected, the investment was indeed a fixed annuity. The generous 4.75% interest rate was only for the first year... to be followed by seven years at an interest rate of 1.25%. They had the flexibility to withdraw their funds whenever they chose, but only by paying a surrender charge of 7%.

Luckily, they consulted me first. I am not making a judgment on the product, which may be right for some people. However, it was not right for David and Anne.

An investor who was not so fortunate

Unfortunately for Florence, she ignored my instructions and failed to check with me *before* agreeing to any investment. She entered my office and proudly informed me of the investment she had made, telling me, "I just invested $50,000 in a tax-free CD that pays 7% interest per year."

"Impossible," I told her.

She insisted that she was correct, saying, "The bank manager herself recommended the product."

Since the branch was only a few blocks from my office, I offered to accompany her to the bank and find out what she had actually purchased. The bank manager was indignant that Florence had brought me along, but finally revealed that Florence had actually "invested" $50,000 to purchase a single-payment life insurance policy.

Florence was 84 years old at the time, a widow with no children. Her closest living relative was her 87-year-old sister, who resided in a nursing home and received Medicaid benefits.

The sister was the beneficiary of the life insurance. Should Florence pass away, the proceeds of the life insurance policy would be appropriated by Medicaid. The manager insisted that Florence knew what she purchased, and since the "10-day free look" period had elapsed, cancelling the life insurance would incur surrender penalties. Florence needed the funds, so her only choice was to cancel the policy. Sadly, she incurred a $5,000 penalty.

Scenarios like Florence's are among the reasons I believe so strongly that an investor should consult with an investment advisor *before* making large investment decisions.

THE TRUSTED ADVISOR

The king's senior advisor, on whom he relied for many years, recently passed away and he was searching for a replacement. He called in his seven deputies and announced that one of them would be promoted to this most senior position. But in order to select one of them, he would give them a test, and whoever passed the test would be selected as the senior advisor.

He handed each deputy a sack of flower seeds and told them to go to a certain field divided into seven plots. They were told to design a garden using only these seeds. The one who achieved the nicest, most beautiful garden after nine months would be chosen as his senior advisor.

The seven deputies immediately took the seeds, whereupon they were taken to the fields. Each one created a beautiful design for the flower garden and began plowing and planting the field.

Six months later, the king came to watch the progress. Of the seven fields, six were beginning to show flowers sprouting from the ground, each with a very impressive and beautiful design.

One of the fields was barren. It had been plowed but there was nothing growing in it. The six deputies looked at the barren field, and among themselves mocked the seventh deputy for his lack of progress.

Three more months passed and the time for the selection had come. When the king came to the fields, six were sprouting beautiful flowers, each field more magnificent than the next with the most imaginative designs and colors. Again, one of the fields, the same one as before, was completely barren. The field was plowed and had some grass growing on it, but nothing else. The king looked around and announced, "I have made my decision. Let us go back to the castle."

With great anticipation, they all returned to the castle and the king announced, "I've made my decision." Each one was thinking that his field was surely the best, and the one with the barren field, of course, was out of the running. How could his barren field even be considered?

To everyone's surprise, when the king made his announcement, it was the deputy with the barren field who was awarded the coveted title of senior advisor to the king. The remaining deputies were completely stunned. "How can that be? Look at our fields!" they exclaimed. "How can you compare our fields to his field? Our fields were gorgeous, and his was completely barren. Why did he win?"

The king smiled and told them that when he gave each deputy a sack of seeds, the seeds were useless, incapable of producing anything. He was testing them to see what they would do at that point. "Obviously," he said, "six of you cheated and brought your own seeds as you were only allowed to use the seeds I gave you. The deputy that I selected obviously did not cheat. He kept to the rules, and in my mind is the most trustworthy person I could have as my senior advisor.

Telling the truth

Compare this parable to a financial advisor who is completely honest with his clients. Instead of just painting glowing pictures of possible future performance and making promises he may not be able to keep, he tells them the truth. A trusted advisor should point out to his clients the pitfalls and the dangers of investment possibilities, and be completely honest with them.

And since the financial advisor will be compensated for his services, it's important to understand exactly how the advisor will be paid. Advisors are generally paid in one of the following ways:

Commissions. Compensation for the sale of investments, insurance and other financial products. The firm that provides the financial product, usually a mutual funds or insurance company, compensates the advisor.

Asset based fees. A percentage of the assets managed on an annual basis.

Fee for plan. The advisor is compensated for developing a financial plan. Fees for implementing the plan may be either commissions or an asset based fee.

My friend Jeffrey, a Certified Public Accountant and advisor, related the following story: A new client, a 64-year-old woman, was referred to his office to have her taxes prepared. She dropped off her documents at his office and asked that he call her after reviewing the paperwork.

Among the documents, he noticed a strange-looking statement. It was printed on perforated paper using an old-fashioned dot-matrix printer. As he had never seen a document like this before, he tried to understand the statement but couldn't make much sense out of it. That one investment represented the client's entire net worth; all her money was invested in it.

Jeffrey called the woman and told her that he had analyzed the statement she provided and the strategy simply did not make sense or meet her goals. He suggested that they meet to review her tax return and discuss diversifying her portfolio to a more conservative strategy.

The woman called him back the next day and told him that she was surprised he didn't understand the investment statement. She had shown it to another accountant who did understand it and she decided that she would have him prepare her tax return instead. She came in later that day to retrieve her papers. As fate would have it, that's the day Bernard Madoff was arrested.

"How can we trust you?"

I had never been asked this question before and wasn't prepared for it, but in the post-Madoff period, it was inevitable. It was my second meeting with Abe and Carol. They clearly felt at ease working with me but were hesitant to sign on as clients and retain me to manage their investments. I sensed their reservations and asked them if they had any concerns.

After a brief pause, Carol asked me the question: "How can we trust you?" They were in their 70s and about to entrust me with their life savings. My job would be to invest their savings to help them pursue a comfortable retirement.

There was no reason for me to be indignant and it was definitely a legitimate question for a client to ask. They weren't questioning my integrity and it wasn't a personal question. I didn't believe that a response vouching for my history of dealing ethically with advising clients with their financial matters over a forty-year period would be satisfactory. After all, until his exposure, Madoff had a long history of dealing "ethically" with people. People, institutions, foundations, and "sophisticated investors" trusted him with their money.

As I was thinking of an appropriate answer, I recalled my clients' constant complaint about the overwhelming amount of mail their investments generated. When Madoff's clients invested money with him, payments were made to *his* firm, and his clients periodically received a single statement generated by *his* office. Madoff was the investment advisor, custodian of the money, and preparer of the statements.

In addition, his "investment strategy" was opaque, i.e., nobody understood his strategy and what they were actually investing in. People entrusted their money with him based solely on his name and the returns he fraudulently reported. As Madoff himself said, "I was astonished. They never even looked at my stock records. If investigators had checked... it would have been easy for them to see. If you are looking at a Ponzi scheme, it's the first thing you do."

The primary focus of the investment advisor is to manage your investments, focusing on the right asset allocation[5] for your objectives and tolerance for risk, and then monitoring your progress toward your goals. You need to have confidence in the advisor and trust him to make the right investment decisions. The performance of the investment is not guaranteed, but the advisor should never have custody of your money.

I explained to Carol, as I do with all my clients, that my service is limited to giving financial guidance and providing advice on selecting the investments. To avoid disasters such as the above and to gain trust in your advisor, the following basic steps should be taken:

- All checks should be made out to, and deposited with, an independent custodian.[6] Never make out a check to the advisor or his personal firm.
- You should be able to check your account on the custodian's website 24/7.
- Your investments should be transparent. The share prices of stocks, bonds and mutual funds in the account can be checked daily online or in newspapers such as the Wall Street Journal.

---

5. Asset allocation does not assure or guarantee better performance and cannot eliminate the risk of investment losses.
6. A custodian is a specialized financial institution that holds customer assets and securities (stocks and bonds) in safekeeping, arranges the settlement of any purchase or sale, and handles deliveries in and out of such securities.

- The description of each stock and the strategy of each mutual fund you own should be fully disclosed, and you should be able to verify this directly on the mutual fund's own website.
- You should be receiving mail directly from the investments you own. Corporations and mutual funds mail annual and semi-annual reports. There may be other mail as well. Your mailbox may become stuffed and reading the material is not required (but advisable). Many clients complain about the amount of mail they receive, and I point out that it's for their benefit. The reports are mandated by law and cannot be halted; however, many mutual funds provide an option to receive them by email.
- The selection of an advisor should include checking his ADV form. The form is available on the SEC website: www.adviserinfo.sec.gov/iapd/content/search/iapd_orgsearch.aspx. The form provides information on his or her education, professional background, any disciplinary problems, lawsuits or arbitration proceedings, investment philosophy, and method of payment. Another source is FINRA's Broker Check: www.finra.org.

Chapter 3

MOVING FORWARD

THE END RESULT BEGINS WITH A PLAN

When my wife and I purchased our first home, we were like all the other young first-time home buyers: short of cash. Our "new" 80-year-old house needed immediate renovations, and somehow we managed to scrape together the funds to make the necessary changes.

We interviewed several contractors, gave them a general idea of what we wanted, and hired the cheapest one. Suffice it to say that we got what we paid for: crooked floors, windows that did not insulate properly, tiles that fell off the walls, and more. I will never forget the phone call from my wife: "Asher," she said, "we have bad news." I was getting used to these surprises. "Steve (the contractor) tried to install a new lighting fixture, but while he was dismantling the old one, the electrical wires disintegrated. He says we must change all the electric wiring in the house."

"How much will it cost?" I asked.

"$8,000," was her reply. And so it went.

The purchase and renovation of our second home was considerably different because we had learned our lesson. This time we hired an engineer and an interior decorator. We hired the best contractor we could find. (The fact that he was also my client helped the situation.) The renovations proceeded smoothly, and although they were more extensive than those of our first home, they took less time to complete. We were very pleased with the results.

The difference between our experiences with the two houses was that in the second case, *we had a plan.*

If you have no idea where you are going, any road will get you there

You never get into a car and start the engine without a destination. We not only have an idea of where we are going, but we have a GPS or road map if we are traveling to unfamiliar territory.

In the same way, all of us need a road map for our finances. Your investment plan should be a carefully planned strategy to pursue your goals. The financial road map is called a personal "Investment Policy Statement" (IPS). This document should:
1) Establish the criteria for your long-term objectives.
2) Provide a frame of reference to help you focus on your long-term objectives. This will be especially important in times of market volatility which may tempt you to react to short-term factors.
3) Establish the criteria to measure your progress.

With the IPS in hand, you will be able to react calmly and intelligently any time your barber offers you a stock tip.

The Investment Policy Statement (IPS) is the most important element of your financial plan and is vital in the successful pursuit of your goals. All future financial decisions will be evaluated and reviewed based on the ground rules established in your IPS.

Similar to designing and following the blueprint of a house, this process involves the planning and the implementation of your plan, with the additional step of meeting periodically with your advisor to monitor and review the progress of the plan. At this time, one may consider any changes that may be necessary should the conditions change.

Your IPS includes:
- Goals and objectives
- Investing time horizon: the length of time before the investment is sold and reverted to cash[1]
- Risk tolerance
- Return requirements
- Income needs
- Liquidity requirements
- Tax and legal considerations

Goals and objectives

Be realistic. If you are 55 years old and have not saved at all for your retirement, you cannot expect to have a million dollars in ten years unless you win the lottery. But I would recommend *not* buying lottery tickets and saving the cost of the tickets. On the other hand, one need not be discouraged. The Investment Policy Statement is a serious and deliberative process. Be practical and set reasonable goals.

A tax client recently came to my office for his annual income tax preparation. He was 52 years old with no savings of his own, but he had just inherited $10,000 which he figured would be his nest egg. He told me his plan and asked that I implement it for his financial security.

He said that he had heard about a stock that had done phenomenally well over the past ten years, returning 90% a year. According to his plan, he would deposit the $10,000 in a brokerage account and give the instruction to purchase stocks that would appreciate a *modest* 30% annually (he would forego the 90% as he was not being greedy). That way, at the time of his retirement in ten years, he would

---

1. See the chapter below entitled "Investment Time Horizon."

have $470,000, sufficient money to live out his days in comfort.

I gave him a dose of reality, as his expectations were unrealistic and I was certain his plan would surely fail. He was insistent that his plan was reasonable, and since we didn't see eye to eye and I could see that I wasn't going to change his mind, I did not accept him as an investment client.

A goal without a plan is just a wish

Rather than daydreaming or engaging in wishful thinking, it is best to start the planning process by answering the following questions:

What is your goal?

Why is this goal important to you?

What will it cost to pursue this goal?

How will you prioritize your goals?

Goals such as "I want to be wealthy," or "I want a comfortable retirement," or even "I want to be debt free" will not do. You must be specific.

Examples might be:
- I want to pay off my credit cards ($12,000) in the next twelve months.
- I want to start a college fund for my son. He is six years old and will need $75,000 when he is eighteen years old.
- Five years from now we will need a down payment for a house; estimated cost: $100,000.
- I want to retire in fifteen years with $1,000,000; I currently have $340,000.
- I want to build an extension on my house; cost: $75,000.
- I want to go on a cruise next summer; cost: $6,000.

Setting goals

It is important to set realistic goals based on factors you can control. If your goal is $1 million at retirement, do not count on a future inheritance or winning the lottery. If your desire is to reduce your credit card balance by paying extra every month on your credit card bill, cut down on your spending.

If you are married, this process must be a joint effort. Begin by listing all your goals, even those unrealistic dreams. Eventually you will narrow your goals to the four or five that are most important, but listing all of them will give you a sense of direction.

Review your list and classify your wishes as **major life-changing goals** (i.e., retirement, house, children's education, or wedding) and **goals of lesser importance** (i.e., debt reduction, car purchase, or vacation). Now select two or three from each category, but no more than a total of five. Dealing with a greater number of goals is impractical, confusing, and can result in your failure to implement the process at all. Life creates many challenges and opportunities, and as we go through many of life's transitions, our attitudes and goals evolve.

Although our priorities change, the majority of us cope financially. Most people have a sense of what is right for them, and they act accordingly. Now it is wise to focus on those few goals where planning can really have an impact. The goals that will not be considered at this point can be addressed at a later time.

To facilitate the process, **list your goals on paper**. The simple act of writing down your goals begins the process of clarifying and classifying them, thereby transforming them into reality.

Listing goals, on paper or on an electronic device, produces an almost magical feeling of becoming more efficient and productive. I discovered this at a Time

Management course that I once attended. At many points in our professional and personal lives, we feel overwhelmed by our responsibilities. As we juggle and prioritize the tasks in our minds, there does not seem to be enough time to accomplish all that is necessary. Stress levels rise and, in fact, we become less productive. The simple act of writing down what needs to be done has an immediate calming effect on many people. The tasks suddenly become less overwhelming and more manageable.

The next step is to investigate the cost of each goal. This step is the most technically challenging and, unless you have the tools and experience to do it, you will probably need the assistance of an advisor.

For example, let's assume you have an investment portfolio worth $150,000. You want to retire in 15 years and you estimate that you will need $1 million for a comfortable retirement. Consider the following questions:

How much should you save monthly?

How much can you afford to invest monthly?

How should the money be invested?

What rate of return should you require for the growth of your portfolio?

The four questions are interrelated. A higher growth rate of your portfolio will result in a lower monthly investment, while a lower growth rate will require greater monthly investments.

Which risk level is acceptable to you?

Based on your risk level, are your goals realistic?

As all the assumptions are based on a goal of $1 million in 15 years, is that goal realistic? Is it too high, or perhaps too low? All your goals should be subject to the same scrutiny.

Since each goal has a price tag and presumably your resources are limited, you must prioritize them. How important is each one to you? Some may be short-term (to pay off debt in two years), while others may be long-term (retirement, higher education). As you assess the goals, you may be motivated and focused on accomplishing some, while deciding to postpone others until a more appropriate time.

With your top three most important goals at hand, let us move on to the next section.

Expectations regarding returns

Hand in hand with making sound investments and taking reasonable educated risks, you must be realistic about your expectations regarding the return on your investments.

Mr. and Mrs. Feldman, "investors" in bank Certificates of Deposit (CDs), came to my office for a financial planning meeting. They were unhappy with the low interest earned on the CDs, and after reviewing their options, agreed to invest 30% of their money in equity mutual funds and 70% in bonds.

A year later, at the annual review of their portfolio, they were dissatisfied with the 8.19% return because the stock market that year was up 15.99%. They were dissatisfied clients, despite the fact that their money was now earning over four times more than when it was in the bank getting only about 2%, outperforming their own benchmark that was based on their risk tolerance. In addition, they were unwilling to accept the risks associated with equities, but wanted stock market returns. What they desired was just not going to happen. It is impossible to have both the safety of CDs (or bonds) and the returns that equities can give you (see example below).

Measure your returns against your benchmark

Assume that your selected portfolio was a "70/30" portfolio: 70% was invested in bonds and 30% in equities. During the year 2014, the return for bonds was 6.00% (as measured by AGG) and 13.46% for equities (as measured by the S&P 500).[2] The benchmark return of your portfolio would then be 8.31% (70% x 6.00% + 30% x 13.69%). Obviously, since a large portion of the portfolio is invested in bonds, it makes no sense to expect to earn equity-like returns.

Do not lose money

Certain foundations of investing sound deceptively simple, especially the cardinal rule: Do not lose money. This principle seems obvious, yet it is critical for successful financial planning or creating an investment strategy. The reason for its special importance is that when one loses money, one must earn all the more money in order to compensate for the loss. If you had $100 and lost 50%, you would have $50 left, but that $50 would have to increase by 100% in order for you to recoup your loss and simply return to your original starting point of owning $100. Recouping 100% is mighty difficult to do.

Therefore, if you can minimize your losses, the gains will generally take care of themselves. A portfolio that is well diversified[3] is a portfolio that may outperform a more aggressive portfolio. For example, an investment portfolio that returns a stable 10% annually will outperform an

---

2. See www.morningstar.com.
3. Any investment portfolio has its ups and downs, but the declines in a diversified portfolio are generally not severe.

    In general, bond prices rise when interest rates fall, and vice versa. This effect is usually more pronounced for longer term securities. You may have a gain or loss if you sell a bond prior to its maturity date.

    Diversification does not assure or guarantee better performance and cannot eliminate the risk of investment losses.

investment portfolio which in one year earns 30% and in the next year loses 10%, even though the simple average of the two would be the same 10%. This principle is clarified by the following two examples:

Example #1: The first year, your investment of $100,000 returned 30%, and at year-end your investment was worth $130,000. In the second year, the investment declined by 10%, or $13,000 (10% of the $130,000) so that the investment was worth $117,000 at the end. Although you averaged a 10% annual return (30% less 10% divided by 2 years), your investment actually increased by only 17% (not 20%).

Example #2: Your investment of $100,000 returned 10% after the first year and your investment appreciated to $110,000. In the second year you also earned 10% on your investment, or $11,000 (10% of $110,000), so that your investment was worth $121,000 at the end. Although you averaged a 10% annual return (10% plus 10% divided by 2 years), your investment actually increased by 21% (not 20%).

Most important is to take action

If there are five frogs on a log and three decided to jump off, how many frogs would be left on the log? Answer: Five. Deciding to do something is not the same as acting on that decision.

The job of a financial advisor is to help a client make a decision and then make sure that that client follows through with the plan. Making a decision is one thing, but ensuring that a client follows through is quite another.

INVESTMENT TIME HORIZON

Subtract your age from 100 and that's how much you should invest in equities. The rest goes into bonds. This is a famous rule of thumb that… doesn't work.

Rose is an 86-year-old retired teacher. Between her New York City pension and Social Security benefits, her income is $75,272. Her living expenses are about $50,000 a year. Should her portfolio of $2,150,000 be allocated so that 85% is invested in bonds? Her three children, ages 56, 58, and 62, will inherit her estate. Rose decided that the portfolio be invested as if the requirements were according to the children's needs.

Alan and Gail are both 30 years old with 3 children and $120,000 in a savings account. Should 70% of their $120,000 savings be allocated to equities? They are in the market for a house and will need the money for a down payment when they find the right one. If they invest the money in equities, even a temporary decline in the market at the "wrong" time will prevent them from having the down payment if the right house is found at that time. Obviously, then, the money should remain in the savings account.

So it was understandable that Gail was frustrated. I could sense it the minute I answered the phone. She wanted to know why her money was "invested" in a money market account where she was only earning 1.45% interest. Didn't she remember that they needed to be liquid in case they found the house of their dreams?

First, I explained to her that the money is not invested in a money market account; it is temporarily deposited there. We deposit funds in money market accounts when we expect that the funds will be needed in the short term. The source of the funds in the money market account was the sale of all their previous investments, as she and her husband were aggressively searching for a home and needed "every single dollar" for the down payment.

Every investment has a risk, and a risk is defined as the chance of experiencing a loss. Even so-called "safe investments" such as government bonds can result in losses should the money be needed before the bond matures. Yes, with 20/20 hindsight – had we known that Gail and her husband would not purchase a house for three years, and that the market would rise – we could have earned a better return. But the lower return was the "opportunity cost" of having the money liquid and safe.

The decision to stay in a money market account over the three-year period "cost" Gail and her husband about $4,800 due to the lower money market rates of 1.45%, so I could not help but chide her about her delay in buying a house. I was aware that Gail was very particular about the house she would buy and turned down a few attractive offers that her husband was willing to accept. "Gail," I asked her, "in the past three years, how much have home prices increased? How much more will it cost you today to buy a house compared with three years ago?" At the other end of the phone I heard a deep sigh.

The term "time horizon" is simply the passage of time needed to reach your goal. Why is it so important to know your investment's time horizon? This horizon will determine how your money will be invested.

As illustrated above, Gail had a perceived short-term time horizon with a zero risk tolerance, so her money was put into a money market account rather than invested into the market. As you move further along the time horizon, you should be able to accept a higher level of risk, which historically has resulted in higher returns. A "higher level of risk" generally implies a larger allocation of the portfolio to equities. Historically, equities have outperformed bonds over longer periods of time.[4]

If you plan to retire in 15 years, your time horizon to meet your financial retirement goals is 15 years. But my experience has shown that investors have their own internal time horizon.

For example, you know you are saving for retirement that may be 15 or 20 years away, so your investment strategy is tilted toward equities and you are determined to stick to your plan and take the "long view"; that is, you will not let the short-term volatility of the markets undermine your strategy.

Then a curious thing happens. You may invest with your mind, but once your money is invested, you start thinking with your heart, or worse, your stomach. You check the mutual fund prices every day, you scrutinize your monthly brokerage statements and note the gains and losses. When the market declines a few days in a row, you become uneasy. When the financial markets begin to tumble or have fallen by a record amount, you worry excessively about losing everything. And when you cannot stand the bad news any longer, you sell. In Wall Street jargon, you have now surrendered or capitulated. You have abandoned long-term strategy in favor of embracing your real time horizon, which is your tolerance for loss. Unfortunately, this final action of selling often signals a market bottom.

Once again, dealing with this aspect of your behavior is the greatest challenge to your financial success. Many advisors emphasize that the solution to this challenge is through education. Education will help investors understand market volatility, and their investments will be set according to their personal tolerance for risk. This will

---

4. Ibbotson® SBBI®, Stocks, Bonds, Bills and Inflation 1926-2013.

enable them to weather a possible decline in the value of their investments.

Secondarily, their trust in their advisor is what enables them to stay the course. Nevertheless, it is wise to remember that the investment should always be structured with an understanding of your own personal nature.

THE RIGHT (AND WRONG) WAY TO INVEST

You feel great. A few weeks ago you decided to invest a portion of your liquid assets (the money that was sitting in the bank), and you purchased mutual funds recommended by a financial magazine.

After just three weeks, the value of your investments has already risen by 5%, more than the bank paid you in a whole year. It is a shame that you only invested a small portion of your money, since the financial gurus on radio and television are bullish and predict that the stock market will continue to increase in value. They say now is the time to increase your exposure to the stock market and you eagerly await the arrival of the new issue of the financial magazine.

As soon as it arrives, you review its new recommendations of stocks and mutual funds, and you buy some of these as well. Now you sit back and wait to enjoy all the wonderful profits. You tell yourself that you should have invested years ago instead of leaving the money in the safety of the bank. In your imagination, you already begin to spend some of your new wealth; in fact, you may even be able to retire sooner than you ever expected.

A week later, something is wrong. The stock market is ignoring the bullish predictions of the "gurus" and is actually declining. That was not supposed to happen. You track your mutual funds daily, and the stocks hourly, and watch as they drop in value. Your new investments are in the red and the 5% gain on the original investment is almost gone. You wish your money was back in the safety of the bank.

What should you do?

You know someone who bought a stock and afterward the company went bankrupt. He lost all his money. You begin to think that this could happen to you. The same gurus who were so bullish only a few weeks ago are now bearish. All your hard-earned money could disappear. You come to the conclusion that you will be better off if you sell those stocks with some losses rather than risk losing everything. You connect to your online broker and with a few clicks of the mouse, you liquidate your portfolio. Whew! Now the money is back in the bank and it is never coming out again....

The above scenario describes most individual investors. With the S&P 500 Index rising, with full dividend reinvestment at an annualized compounded rate of 11.20% for the past 70 years (January 1945 through December 2014) and 7.45% without dividend reinvestment,[5] why do most people retain the majority of their money at the banks, earning a small fraction of what the stock market could earn them?

The answer can be illustrated with the following story:

August 2000. Albert and Helen were not clients of mine but came to discuss their portfolio and solicit my opinion. It was obvious that Helen was in charge. Their portfolio was valued at $500,000 and was fully invested in equity mutual funds. Albert was 60 years old at the time. Did I think their portfolio could grow to the $1 million they estimated they

---

5. www.politicalcalculations.blogspot.com, "S&P at Your Fingertips."

would need in five years when Albert planned to retire? In order to maintain their lifestyle, they would need about $100,000 a year during retirement. A $1 million portfolio earning 10% per year should be sufficient.

A quick look at their portfolio revealed what I expected. Helen was the financial *"maven,"*[6] and their portfolio included all the popular mutual funds that were receiving media attention. It was loaded with large-cap growth funds that invested in fast-growing companies, and technology funds that invested exclusively in technology stocks.

As I began to discuss the concept of risk and diversification, I quickly realized that Helen was not interested. Although Albert was interested in what I had to say, she considered herself the financial "wizard" of the family and it was apparent that Helen only wanted me to acknowledge her financial acumen to her husband. I concluded the meeting by congratulating her for selecting the mutual funds she had purchased. After all, they were the best performing funds in their asset class (large-cap growth funds and technology funds) which at the time were outperforming all other asset classes. She left the meeting beaming.

October 2002. Albert called again to schedule an appointment. I had no doubt as to what happened to their portfolio during the prior 21 months, but I was still surprised by their story.

The portfolio was now worth only $315,000, and retirement appeared farther in the future than ever. Helen, who listened constantly to radio programs for the latest financial advice, had called a brokerage firm that was advertising heavily on the radio and arranged to meet with a representative. Not surprisingly, the broker advised them to sell all their mutual funds and buy bonds. After all, he

---

6. A Yiddish word for "expert."

told them, "We are in a bear market, and you need the safety of bonds." Again, they were seeking my opinion, except this time, both were willing to listen to my strategy.

I told them it was wrong to get out of the market completely. I recommended a diversified portfolio that included some bonds, but stressed that it should definitely include equities (stocks). I explained to them that markets go through cycles, and fortunately – although we were in the midst of an exceptionally severe down market – the decline in stocks has historically been temporary and I was confident that they would rise again. "You want to be invested when the market recovers. You suffered through the worst of it; just wait a little longer."

The next day, Albert called to tell me that Helen sold all the funds, but wanted me to give her a call to discuss implementing my strategy. When I called, Helen asked me if I have any "good bond funds that pay 8%-9% a year." At the time, bonds were paying about 4%. I wished her luck and with regret, I ended the call.

When I met Albert two years later, he told me that most of their money was in "safe" bonds. Unfortunately, they missed the ensuing stock market recovery.

In my opinion, people who invest in the latest, media-touted financial products tend to do poorly because they are only seeing the trees and not the forest. A seasoned, certified financial planner has knowledge, experience and perspective in the "forest" of finance to help clients avoid the dangerous pitfalls of short-sightedness.

The First Step: Understanding Risk

"The structural stability of the building is the most crucial consideration in designing a building," says my brother Meir, a professional engineer specializing in the construction industry. Meir's job is to implement the architect's design in a way that ensures occupant safety and the integrity of the building. Of course, safety always takes precedence over aesthetics. When asked how he applies structural integrity measures, Meir points to the locality's building code.

A building code is a set of rules that specify the minimum acceptable level of safety for buildings and other structures. It is also stress tested for its effectiveness in withstanding potential adverse conditions such as earthquakes and hurricanes. The main purpose of the building code is to protect public health, safety, and general welfare as they relate to the construction and occupancy of buildings and structures. Building codes vary widely among localities; for example, California's concern about earthquakes is different from Florida's fear of hurricanes, and each develops codes based on its needs.

Likewise, designing your investment portfolio should begin by clarifying your own "building codes" or creating your own "stress test." Financial advisors refer to this as your risk profile. Individuals differ in their financial needs and temperaments. The only truism regarding investments is that they *will* fluctuate in value, and your behavior during stressful periods will ultimately determine the success (or failure) of your strategy.

In establishing your financial strategy, the starting points to consider are two types of risk-related concepts. One is psychological and is known as risk tolerance. The other refers to your financial needs or capacity to take the financial risks that will allow you to pursue your goals. These two concepts are distinct and need to be understood clearly before making investment decisions. Together, the two help to determine the amount of risk that should be taken in an investment portfolio.

Simply put, there are two questions to ask in order to determine how much risk a person should assume in his or her portfolio:
1) Risk Tolerance: "How much risk can you handle psychologically?"
2) Risk Capacity: "How much risk should you assume to meet your financial goals?"

Risk tolerance

Risk tolerance is the amount of risk you are comfortable taking or the degree of downward volatility that you are able to handle. Although risk tolerance often varies with age, income, and financial goals, it is deeply psychological and often affected by life and family experiences. One's risk tolerance is generally determined by questionnaires (see Appendix B) designed to reveal the level at which an investor can invest but still be able to sleep at night.

In my experience, however, questionnaires are inadequate by themselves and should be used in conjunction with an in-depth discussion with your financial planner. The reason is that in the questionnaires, the questions asked are hypothetical and investors are often emotionally detached from the answers they give. In real life, though, when faced with adversity, investors often act differently than they themselves expected. Reaction to experiencing an actual portfolio drop of 20% is much different from asking hypothetically how you would feel about it.

Risk tolerance measures your willingness to accept higher risk or volatility in exchange for potentially higher returns. During a market downturn, an individual with a higher tolerance for risk might not sell his stocks (or he may even buy stocks), while a person averse to risk might panic and sell at the wrong time.

While risk tolerance is a measure of how much risk you can emotionally or psychologically handle, it is not necessarily a measure of the appropriate amount of risk you should take.

Risk capacity

Risk capacity determines the amount of risk that you need to take in order to pursue your financial goals, and conversely, the ability to withstand a fall in value and the consequences of a loss of capital income.

Rather than dealing with a subjective emotional factor used to determine risk tolerance, risk capacity is more quantitative and can be measured. You start with the rate of return necessary to reach your goals by estimating your time horizon and income requirements. With this information, you can decide upon the types of investments to use and the level of risk to assume.

Balancing risk

The challenge to investors (and advisors) in crafting an investment strategy is that for many investors, risk tolerance and risk capacity are not the same. The investor may not be willing to accept the level of risk necessary to help him pursue his goals, and when risk tolerance is higher than necessary, unnecessary risk could mistakenly be taken. Every investment has a risk of a loss. Even if you can tolerate and/or afford to have your investments decline in value, why risk it if it's unnecessary?

In assessing a client's risk profile, the way the questions are framed is important. For example, I'll ask, "If you invest $500,000 and the market fluctuates or is volatile, and if you assume that in a year from now, your $500,000 drops by 10%, is that acceptable? Can you tolerate it and stay with the plan?"

They usually respond, "Yes, we can tolerate a 10% loss. We understand that the usual decline is temporary because historically, the market recovers and reaches even higher levels."

I then change the question: "What if you invest $500,000, and a year from now the value of your portfolio is only worth $450,000? Is that acceptable to you?" Usually they answer, "No, we can't afford a $50,000 decline. We don't want to take such a risk."

On paper, 10% is no more than a statistic. However, 10% of $500,000 is $50,000, and when people consider it as actual money, they tend to value the $50,000 in a completely different way.

> *You need to acknowledge and state your level of risk in terms of actual money.*

New clients usually start our meeting by saying, "We would like to make good investments, but we do not want to take a risk." My response is, "How do you define risk?" The usual answer is, "We do not want to lose any money."

Risk tolerance and risk capacity were discussed above, but what other risks are considered in developing an investment portfolio?

There are two types of risks: financial market risks and personal lifestyle risks, and each can be divided into many categories. However, the main difference between the two is that you have no direct control over financial market risks, while you can, to a great degree, reduce or eliminate personal lifestyle risks by modifying your actions and behavior, as will be addressed at the end of the chapter.

Financial market risks

Inflation risk: This is the risk that your investment will not maintain its purchasing power due to the increase in the cost of living. Investments subject to inflation risk include cash sitting in your checking account, bank CDs, and bonds (U.S. government, municipal, corporate and international).

To begin the discussion of inflation risk, let's look at the example of a fictitious man named Irving:

Irving was born 65 years ago (in 1949), and since earliest childhood he remembers his father telling him, "Irving, you do not have to worry about your retirement; I have secured it for you. I have put aside sufficient funds for you in a very safe place so that when you retire, you will have enough to last you for the rest of your life. Enjoy life. Trust me, you don't ever have to put aside another penny."

So Irving lived the good life. He worked but never saved because he trusted his father and believed that he had enough money with which to retire and live a most comfortable life. Accordingly, at age 65, Irving announced his retirement and went to the bank to recover the retirement money his father had set aside for him.

The bank officer brought him a nice-sized deposit box where Irving found $93,600 in cash. This was the total sum his father had left him to last the rest of his life. In 1949, the median income in the United States was about $3,120, so he left him enough money ($93,600) to last 30 years. According to the Social Security Administration, the median income in 2013 was $44,888. Irving's $93,600 would not even begin to support him during his longed-for retirement.

Can we say Irving lost any money? No, we cannot. His parents had put away $93,600 for him, and he still owned the $93,600. Was putting money in a safe deposit box risky? It all depends on how one defines risk.

As an exercise, take a bill from your wallet – the denomination doesn't matter – and describe what you are holding. Your likely answer would be that it is money. But what you are actually holding is currency. That piece of paper is a means of exchange. You will exchange the bill, whether it is ten or a hundred dollars, for goods or services of equivalent value. The denomination of the currency defines its purchasing power. The bill you are holding purchases less than it did ten years ago, and probably more than it will ten years from now, due to inflation.

Since 1949, the annual rate of inflation averaged 3.52%,[7] reducing the purchasing power of the $93,600 to only $9,239 in 2014. By 2014, Irving would need $923,858 in order to maintain the purchasing power the $93,600 had in 1949.

For the 65-year period, 1949 thru 2014, the S&P 500 returned an average annualized return of 11.38% (with dividends reinvested).[8] In 1949, it was not possible to invest in a mutual fund or ETF that tracked the S&P 500 Index, but an investment of $93,600 in MFS Massachusetts Investors Trust Class A (MITTX) in January 1, 1949 would grow to $68,567,115 by March 31, 2015.[9] (Please note that past performance does not guarantee future results; that the investment return and principal value of an investment will fluctuate so that an investor's shares, when redeemed, may be worth more or less than their original cost; and that

---

7. See www.politicalcalculations.blogspot.com, "S&P at Your Fingertips."
8. Ibid.
9. MFS Investment Management, June 11, 2015. The performance of the fund for quarter ended 3/31/2015 was 1.25, 1 year 10.82, 5 years 13.07, 10 years 8.49. Gross expense ratio is 0.78.

current performance may be lower or higher than the performance data quoted.)

If an investment does not allow you to maintain its purchasing power, then by definition it would cause you to lose money. Let's use a bank CD as an example. You open a 5-year bank CD and lock it in at an annual rate of 4% for 5 years, at which time the principal is guaranteed to be returned to you. The CD pays you 4% today, but inflation is 3% so you will only have earned 1%. To make matters worse, you will pay a 30% tax on the 4%, so that your after-tax return will be 2.8%. After an inflation factor of 3%, your actual return will be a negative 0.2%. Thus, your supposedly risk-free investment actually locks in annual losses! Maybe one could say that "CD" stands for "Certain Depreciation" of assets.

Inflation is a major concern that people need to consider in their long-term planning. Today's 65-year-old retirees are facing a possible 30-plus years in retirement, and the cost of living may triple over their next 30 years of life. An investment strategy that maintains the portfolio's purchasing power is the greatest challenge. Over the very long run, the stock market has had an inflation-adjusted annualized return rate of between 6%-7%,[10] and it is my opinion that equities should be considered for inclusion in every portfolio.

Other important terms

> **Market Risk:** This is the risk that the value of your investment will decline. Stock and bond prices change continuously (some every second) when the markets are open. And *every* investment is subject to market risk. Stocks, bonds, real estate, gold, and commodities are each subject to their own specific types of market risk.

---

10. See www.politicalcalculations.blogspot.com, "S&P at Your Fingertips."

Default Risk: This is the risk that your investment will become worthless. U.S. government bonds and bank accounts (under $250,000 and FDIC insured) are not subject to such risk. Ownership of actual gold coins is also not subject to default risk. Investment grade municipal bonds have a minor risk, as does real estate (for example, there is a small chance that one could discover a toxic waste dump under one's home).

Credit Risk: This is the risk that the financial institution issuing bonds will decline and might eventually default on its obligations. Financial institutions are rated by credit rating agencies, with AAA indicating the most financially secure. Higher-rated companies pay a lower interest rate than do those with a lower rating.

Interest Rate Risk: This is the risk that interest rates will increase. Investors and professionals closely monitor the Federal Reserve's actions, as interest rates affect almost all the investments we make.

Adjustable-rate mortgages are adversely affected by interest rates because a rise in interest rates results in higher monthly interest on mortgage payments, potentially causing homeowners to default. A rise in interest rates will also result in falling bond values. Long-term bonds are affected more significantly than short-term bonds. For example, following a 1% increase in interest rates after you've bought the bond – should you decide to sell it prior to its maturity date – there may be a 10% decline in a 30-year bond, but only a 4% drop in a bond maturing in five years. Professionals call this an inverse relationship between the value of the bond and the interest rate; that is, as interest rates increase, bond values decrease, and vice versa.

Imagine, for example, that you purchased a $100,000 U.S. government 30-year bond that pays 4%. The U.S. government promises to pay you 4% – that is, $4,000 – in interest every year for the next 30 years. At the end of the 30 years, the government will return your investment of $100,000. You have made the safest investment possible, and it is guaranteed by the "full faith and credit of the U.S. government."

Let's say a year after you made your investment, interest rates increase to 5% but you are still receiving your $4,000 (4%). When rates rise to 6% the following year and you are still receiving the same $4,000, you feel foolish and decide to sell those 4% bonds and exchange them for better-yielding bonds. You cannot sell them back to the government, which will only buy back the bonds at maturity, which could be 10-30 years from their date of issuance. Therefore, you decide to sell them through a broker on the "open market."

No one, however, will pay $100,000 for a bond that pays 4% when new bonds are paying 6%. So if you were to sell that bond (yielding 4%), you'll receive about $80,000. Here is the reasoning: The annual interest payment of $4,000 will now compute as 5% of $80,000 and since, at the end of the 30 years, the buyer will receive $100,000, he will earn an additional $20,000, for a total annual return of 6%. Of course, you can keep the bond until the time of maturity, but you will only earn 4% while everyone around you is earning more. Our example dispels the myth that there is no way to lose money on government bonds.

Prepayment Risk: This is the risk that your principal will be returned to you earlier than expected. This usually affects bonds in a falling interest environment. Imagine you purchased a 20-year bond that pays 6% annual interest. Interest rates decline to 4%. Unbeknownst to you, the bond has a "call feature": The issuing financial institution has the right to "call in" the bond and pay you its face value at any time. You now have the unpleasant opportunity to reinvest your money at a lower rate.

Currency Risk: This is the risk that the currency exchange rates will fluctuate. Investing overseas exposes you to such a risk. For example, if you invest in European stocks, a 6% decline in the Euro relative to the dollar will result in a 6% decline in the value of the investment when the stocks are sold and exchanged for dollars. This risk can be managed by investing in mutual funds that hedge their currency exposure.

Opportunity Risk (also termed Opportunity Cost): This is the risk that an investment you made will prevent you from investing in another opportunity for a higher return. Alternatively, it is the cost of inaction and lost opportunity. If you keep your money in a savings account for a year when you could have invested it in a stock that will rise considerably that year, you will suffer an opportunity cost.

Taxes: Although not a risk, taxes do limit your upside potential. The government, while a major partner in your gains, will not be there for you when you lose.

Paul was seething when he left my office. He invested his life savings in a real estate venture and, after a gut-wrenching experience, made a profit of $3.2 million. A few days after he sold the property (and celebrated his success), he came to my office to review the financial consequences of the sale. I tried to be as gentle as possible while informing him that he owed about $1 million in taxes (federal, state and local taxes combined). I could literally see the blood drain from his face. "How can that be?!" he exclaimed. "After all the risks I took? At times it looked like I would lose my entire investment. And I provided work for so many people!"

There is very little one can do to prevent financial market risks. As you can see, every investment you make has some element of risk. But not all investments are subject to the same risk.

Although you cannot avoid risk, you can learn to manage it

Tommy is learning about risk management. I first met Tommy in October, 2006. A brilliant, methodical 22-year-old, he quit college and began day trading in stocks. Day trading generally refers to the practice of buying and selling stocks within the same trading day. Active day traders involved in high-volume trading may trade up to several hundred orders a day.

Despite his brilliance, Tommy was financially ruined within a few months. In the process of reassessing his future, he was introduced to the foreign exchange market (forex). In an effort to learn from his mistakes, Tommy took his time to study the currency markets and develop a trading strategy. When he was ready, he raised $10,000 from his family.

By the time he called me, Tommy had been trading currencies for about six months and his account had grown to an unbelievable $148,000. The purpose of our meeting was twofold. One, he needed a CPA to help him with some tax planning. "I estimate that by year end, my account will be over $300,000," he confidently forecast. And his second request: "I am also looking for investors who will invest with me. Even though currency trading can be very risky, I have developed a strategy to hedge the risk and can offer people a return of 80%-100% per year with minimum risk." I had heard promises like this before. Rather than engaging in costly tax planning ideas, I made some suggestions and told him to return in January when we could calculate the sum to set aside for the taxes due by April 15.

We met again during the first week in January, 2007. When Tommy showed me his income for the year, I was surprised that his profits had dwindled to $42,000. In comparison with the magnitude of this loss, tax planning became a minor issue. "Tommy, what happened?" I asked him. "During the week of Thanksgiving," he answered, "the currency markets became volatile in ways that I had not predicted. Within five days, I lost about $100,000. But now, I have refined my strategy so that if this happens again, I will be ready."

"Tommy, that is not adequate," I told him. "You have to plan for the risk that you have *not* thought about."

Personal financial risks – a short questionnaire

1. What would be the impact on your family's finances if you did not wake up tomorrow, G-d forbid?
2. What would be the impact on your family's finances if you could not work because of a disability?
3. Are your children at risk for not attending the college or secondary school program of their choice due to the lack of funds for tuition?
4. Are your own finances at risk because you may need to intervene on behalf of your parents' medical and long-term care needs?
5. When you retire, is your lifestyle at risk because you did not save sufficiently to assure a comfortable retirement?
6. Are you at risk of outliving your money?

7. Are your heirs at risk of forfeiting a large portion of their inheritance to estate taxes?

Controlling your personal risks

Unlike market risks, you can, to a large degree, control your personal risks. Purchasing sufficient life insurance will allow your family to maintain their lifestyle in the event of your death. A disability policy will help in the event that you are unable to work due to a disability.

A successful and wise man, Jonas Ehrlich, advised me to insure myself "to the maximum." He told me, "I sleep well at night. I give the insurance companies money and let them worry about it in case something happens to me or my properties."

If your resources are limited, you may not be able to fully protect yourself against every possible risk, but at least some risks may be reduced or eliminated.

However, regardless of your current financial well-being, it is important to start thinking and planning for your future. Are you saving enough for your retirement? Are you maximizing your contributions to tax-deferred plans? Have you estimated how much money you will need in retirement? And, if you are already in retirement and drawing funds from your investments, are the withdrawals excessive?

The financial quality of your retirement depends on four factors you can control before and during retirement:
1. How much will you save and invest?
2. How long will your money grow?
3. How will you invest your money?
4. Will you be disciplined and stay with the plan?

Do you have a will? Have you consulted with a competent attorney specializing in trusts and estates? Using anyone but a specialist in trusts and estates to draft your will or advise you on estate matters is not recommended.

A financial plan involves more than simply deciding how to invest your portfolio. In fact, investment decisions should not be made until you have considered the above.

Asset Allocation

> "A person should divide up his wealth into three parts: one part in land, one part in merchandise, and one part in liquid capital."
> — Talmud, Bava Metzia 42a

The famous musician

The entire town had gathered at the railroad station to welcome their most prominent citizen, a young man who had gone to the big city to study music and had become the world's foremost musician on his instrument.

"There he is!" cried the mayor as he rushed to give him an official welcome and lead him to the podium erected in his honor. "We are very proud," he said to the famous musician. "Very proud!"

Then, after the speeches, he respectfully asked the now famous young man if he would play some music for them.

"No, I'm sorry," said the young man in a similar respectful tone.

The mayor became flustered. "But why?"

"This is a special instrument," said the young man. "Its purpose is to be played with an orchestra."

But the mayor persisted, and the people persisted.

So the young man reluctantly took out his instrument, and the townspeople sat back to enjoy the beautiful music that he would play.

"This will be wonderful!" the mayor assured them, enjoying the fruits of their persistence.

But when the famous musician began to play, they all slapped their hands to their ears in horror because the noise sounded like the braying of an elephant! After they could not endure the unpleasant sounds anymore, they all begged him to stop.

"Is this a joke, young man?" the mayor demanded. "You are a world-famous musician!"

"Yes, I am," said the young man, shrugging, "But when I play the tuba, it must be within the context of an orchestra. The tuba, all by itself, can sound like just – noise."

A symphonic portfolio

Consider your portfolio as a symphony orchestra: your investments are the instruments that you and your conductor (in this case, your money manager) coordinate so they all play in harmony.

Without the right combination of instruments, it is all just noise. An investment portfolio must have the right mix of investments in order to be effectively diversified. Asset allocation is the diversification, or spreading out, of your investment among stocks, bonds, cash and other non-correlated investments.[11] Cash can be put into very liquid financial instruments like CDs, money market accounts, or very short-term government notes.

Asset allocation is a disciplined approach to portfolio management based on the concept of Modern Portfolio

---

11. Correlation is a statistical measure of how two securities move in relation to each other. Non-correlated investments refer to investments that move differently from each other. For example, commodities are not correlated to stocks, so that when stocks decline, commodities may increase in value.

Theory. The developers of this theory, Harry Markowitz and William Sharpe, were awarded the Nobel Prize in Economic Science in 1990 for their contributions. Modern Portfolio Theory is a revolutionary view of portfolio investment that illustrates how investment risk may be reduced by spreading investments in specific proportions among different asset classes. This strategic approach to investment management is designed to help investors maximize expected returns while attempting to minimize the risk associated with routine market fluctuations.

Developing an investment strategy personalized to your needs and goals begins with asset allocation, the most fundamental and foundational component of portfolio management. Asset allocation means dividing assets among the various asset classes such as stocks and bonds, and alternatives such as real estate, commodities, precious metals, and cash. Each asset class has associated risks as well as potential rewards. These vary based on the anticipated level of exposure over time to market volatility, i.e., the degree to which returns vary within a given time-period.

While there is no single investment product or asset class that eliminates all potential risks – even cash carries the potential risk of failing to outpace inflation over time – how assets are allocated within an investment portfolio has a profound impact on potential risk reduction and the pursuit of more consistent returns. The reason is that different asset classes tend to perform differently at different times. Because of this, when one is up, the other may be down. The combination of asset classes may reduce portfolio volatility.

According to academic studies, the success of your investment will not depend on which individual stocks or mutual funds you buy, but the manner in which you spread out your investments and orchestrate them all. Research shows that smart asset allocation accounts for 93.6% or more of the expected investment returns. Correct market timing and other factors account for only 6.4% of success.[12]

Identifying possible "instruments" in a diversified portfolio

Equity (i.e., stocks) strategies include investing in growth or value funds, large or small company stocks, geographic diversification between domestic (U.S.) and international (non-U.S.) stocks, and choosing to invest in particular sectors, such as real estate through publicly traded real estate investment trusts. (See Appendix C for the description of asset classes.)

Bond diversification includes short-term and long-term bonds, investment-grade or lower-quality "junk" bonds, and foreign bonds.

Similarly, a portfolio that includes a number of stocks, but all in one particular field, is not a balanced portfolio. In 2000, investors who invested all their money into "dot com" stocks lost a great deal of money because they put all their eggs into one basket.

A study by William Goetzmann and Alok Kumar[13] examined over 40,000 equity investment accounts at a large discount brokerage firm during a six-year period and found that the least diversified group of investors suffered the biggest loses. Success lies not in how many stocks one holds, but in the breadth of one's portfolio. An under-diversified portfolio will generally underperform a well-diversified one.

A fascinating advantage of diversifying an investment portfolio is that while it reduces the risk, it does not necessarily reduce the returns. For this reason,

---

12. Brinson, Singer and Bebower, "Determinant of Portfolio Performance II."
13. "Diversification Decisions of Individual Investors and Asset Prices."

diversification is referred to as the only "free lunch" in finance.

An investment strategy includes the trade-off between risk and return. Often the investor assumes that by accepting a greater risk, he can expect a greater return. He thinks he can outsmart or out-time the market. He yearns to invest heavily in the popular stock of the moment and wishes to see immediate gains. In contrast, the professional money manager's first and foremost consideration before making an investment is the risk involved.

The prudent, time-tested road to success comes by allocating your portfolio among stocks, bonds, real estate, cash and possibly commodities. In this way you can target the level of return you wish for each specific risk you are willing to take. Stocks provide the highest returns, but they carry the greatest risk. Bonds are less risky than stocks, but they provide lower returns. Cash is risk free, but barely keeps up with inflation, while real estate and commodities may provide protection from inflation.

A helpful warning

The following chapters on "Rebalancing to Remain on Course" and "Investor Behavior" discuss the two most important components with the greatest impact on your portfolio.

But first a warning.

A well-diversified portfolio means that at any given time, you might have to invest in assets that are underperforming at the moment, or even experiencing negative returns. Keep in mind that this is by design: the same asset that is underperforming now might be the big performer in the near future.

The primary reason to diversify your portfolio is that it is impossible to time the stock market – to know with certainty which stocks and/or sectors will perform best in the future.

If one thinks that playing the market looks fun and exciting, one must bear in mind that the market is as unpredictable as the weather.

I posed an interesting question to my son-in-law's father, Yonatan Goodman, a musical composer and arranger: "In a symphony orchestra comprised of between 10-20 instruments," I asked, "which method will produce better music:

a) "Include all instruments and employ musicians who are of professional caliber, but who play only 80% as well as the finest world-class musicians; or

b) "Omit several instruments, but employ only the finest world-class musicians?"

Yonatan Goodman answered, "You will have a better musical effect if you include all the instruments."

The analogy to portfolio diversification is clear. But asset allocation is only the beginning.

REBALANCING TO REMAIN ON COURSE

As the markets rise and fall, your asset allocation may shift with them, making your portfolio more conservative or more aggressive than what you initially intended. To keep your investment on track, a periodic review should be conducted in order to determine if your portfolio needs to be rebalanced to keep you on course with your stated objectives. If your investments have drifted too far from their targeted portfolio percentages, there may be a need to rebalance your portfolio by selling those funds that have increased in value and buying more of those funds that have fallen in value.

Through rebalancing your portfolio, there is an added benefit of reducing the influence of emotion on investment decisions, as rebalancing seeks to manage the "balance" of your portfolio through the implementation of a disciplined strategy of buying low and selling high.

Here is a simple example. It was determined that Peter's proper allocation, based on his risk tolerance, risk capacity, and goal, should be as follows:

Portfolio Allocation: Beginning of year

Equity fund	60%	$ 60,000
Bond fund	30%	$ 30,000
Cash	10%	$ 10,000
		$100,000

At the end of the year, the equity portion of the portfolio substantially outperformed the bond and treasury portions. This caused an increase in the percentage allocated to the equity fund while decreasing the percentage allocated to the bond and treasury funds.

Portfolio Allocation: End of year

Equity fund	65.1%	$ 78,000
Bond fund	26.3%	$ 31,500
Cash	8.6%	$ 10,300
		$119,800

At year end, the percentage allocated to equities increased to a level that could make Peter uncomfortable with the increased risk associated with that higher percentage. To maintain the original asset allocation strategy, he may sell $6,120 of the equity fund and purchase $4,440 and $1,680 of the bond and treasury funds respectively.

Rebalanced Portfolio Allocation: End of year

Equity fund	60%	$ 71,880
Bond fund	30%	$ 35,940
Cash	10%	$ 11,980
		$119,800

Considerations in rebalancing a portfolio

There are costs to rebalancing. Trading increases costs. Selling stocks, bonds or funds can trigger taxable capital gains, and gains realized on investments held for less than a year (short-term) are taxable at a higher rate than those held for more than a year (long-term).

Review the holding period of the investment; for example, if the holding period of the investment you want to sell at a gain is less than a year, consider delaying the sale until you reach the 12-month holding period. The tax savings can be substantial. But you should only delay the sale if you are confident that the investment will not decline while you are waiting.

Rebalancing can also be accomplished by adding more cash flow to the account either with new cash or cash generated by earned dividends.

A rebalancing threshold should be set; for example, it's time to rebalance when the equity fund increases 5% above the selected allocation.

Frequent rebalancing is generally unnecessary and may be counterproductive, considering the costs, i.e., taxes and transactional costs. The best practice is to rebalance annually unless the previously determined threshold has been penetrated.

Discipline a must

The key term in rebalancing is *discipline*. Rebalancing forces you to buy low and sell high. You will be selling the best performing fund (or asset class) and buying the poorest performers. You'll be taking action that is counter to human behavior. And that is difficult.

You'll be tempted to resist taking action, or even adding to the winners. That could be a mistake, as past performance is not always an indication of future performance. Indeed, some research indicates that the best performers may lag in the future since investments tend to "regress to the mean."[14] In finance, "regression to the mean" is the tendency for assets showing periods of higher returns to be followed by periods of lower returns. For example, the average long-term annual returns for an asset class may be 10%. High-return periods greater than 10% may be followed by periods of lower return.

INVESTOR BEHAVIOR...

...is the most important determinant to the future success of the investment.

---

14. See www.advisorperspectives.com, "Regression to Trend: A Perspective on Long-Term Market Performance," by Doug Short, February 2, 2015.

"Successful investing calls not so much for some clairvoyant ability to read the future [but] for the courage to stick to time-tested, common-sense policies in the face of unreliable emotional stresses and strains that constantly sweep the market place." —George Putnam, 1937

Bull markets are born on pessimism, grow on skepticism, mature on optimism and die on euphoria. Diversify your investments. —John Templeton 1912-2008

Listening to the one who knows better: The fur dealer and the Rebbe

The following is a true story about a partnership between a fur dealer and the Lubavitcher Rebbe. The Rebbe needed the capital to continue building the physical and spiritual infrastructure of Jewish life around the world, and coached an unlikely candidate to help him do it.

"Would you take me as a partner in your business?"

Max Kotz, a member of the Lubavitch Jewish community in England, was shocked by the Rebbe's question. For the Rebbe to be his business partner! Never in his wildest fantasies would he have dreamed of being made such an offer. He immediately agreed.

The Rebbe took out a token sum of dollars and gave it to Mr. Kotz as his investment. "In a partnership," he reminded Mr. Kotz, "neither partner should engage in a deal without the okay of the other. Do you agree?"

Mr. Kotz, an international fur dealer, was somewhat puzzled. What did the Rebbe know about furs? But he agreed. The Rebbe then advised him to purchase large quantities of a particular type of fur.

Mr. Kotz returned to England and invested several thousand dollars in the type of fur the Rebbe had suggested. When he advised the Rebbe of the purchase, the Rebbe answered that his *investment had been far too conservative; a much larger quantity of fur should have been purchased.* And so it went, back and forth, until on the Rebbe's urging, Mr. Kotz had purchased truly astronomical quantities of the desired fur, investing his entire personal fortune and even borrowing large sums.

To Mr. Kotz's surprise, the value of the fur that the Rebbe had advised him to buy began to plummet. Perhaps, he thought, he should sell at least some of the fur he had purchased. As promised, he contacted the Rebbe before making the sale. To his surprise, the Rebbe reminded him that, as partners, it was possible to sell only when both agreed, and at this time, the Rebbe continued, he did not agree to the sale.

The price of the fur continued to sink. And with it sank Mr. Kotz's spirits; it seemed to him that he would certainly be ruined. He contacted the Rebbe repeatedly, but always received the same answer: Don't sell! Worried about his financial future, he finally began to question his entire relationship with the Rebbe and Lubavitch. Perhaps it was all a mistake?

For several months, the price of the fur Mr. Kotz had purchased remained low. But then it suddenly began to rise. When it reached a level at which the loss was bearable, Mr. Kotz again consulted the Rebbe. "Maybe it's time to sell?" But still the Rebbe refused. Again there followed a chain of telephone calls from Mr. Kotz to the Rebbe's office as the price of the fur steadily advanced. At each juncture, Mr. Kotz desired to sell, and always the Rebbe advised him to wait.

As the price of the fur continued to rise, Mr. Kotz's trust in the Rebbe also returned. Only when the price of the fur had doubled did the Rebbe finally agree that the time had come to sell. In a relatively short time, Mr. Kotz was able to sell his entire inventory at a resounding profit. Even after repaying the loans and calculating his costs, he had still made millions.

It was time, thought Mr. Kotz, to give his partner his share. At **yechidus** *(a private meeting),* the Rebbe declined to take a penny, instructing Mr. Kotz to donate the Rebbe's share to different charitable causes throughout the world.

"Would you like to continue as partners?" Mr. Kotz asked hopefully. The Rebbe, however, demurred. "You're a shvacher shutaf, *a weak-hearted partner*," he replied.

This story illustrates an example of the fluctuating trust an investor can have in his advisor in times of doubt. Although this story pushes that expectation of trust to an extreme, the story serves as a good analogy for one's emotional roller coaster during times of market fluctuation. It is only fair, however, to note that a financial advisor will never have the Divinely inspired vision of a spiritual leader such as the Rebbe, but the point stands. To weather the highs and lows of market trends, one could do well to trust a professional advisor and ride the waves together.

(This story is based on the teachings of the Lubavitcher Rebbe, adapted by Rabbi Eli Touger in Keeping In Touch, Vol 2. *Published by Sichos in English, sie.org.)*

THE MIND RULES THE HEART

The tale of the cat and mouse

A Rabbi was summoned to the king to debate with his advisors. The topic was, what has a greater influence on a person's behavior: logic (i.e., that which can be taught through intellect) or his nature?

The advisors argued that logic has a greater influence, while the Rabbi was of the opinion that it is a person's nature. Following an intense debate, the king was unable to declare a winner and ordered the opposing sides to appear before him in one month's time to bring additional proof to bolster their opinion.

The Rabbi returned to his studies and quickly forgot about the debate. A month later, the king's messengers arrived to transport the Rabbi to the castle. The Rabbi gathered his books into a bag and took it with him to the castle. Unbeknownst to the Rabbi, a mouse was hiding in the bag.

At the castle, the king's advisors prepared their demonstration to prove their theory. They presented a cat, dressed as a butler and trained to walk on its hind legs while carrying a tray of full wine glasses. Amazingly, the cat carried the tray without spilling a drop.

The king was impressed and was about to declare his advisors the winners of the debate when the mouse suddenly ran out of the Rabbi's bag. Spotting the mouse, the cat immediately forgot all its training, dropped the tray with the wine glasses, and began chasing the mouse.

You can train an animal to do amazing things, but at the end of the day, a cat is a cat.

Now can human *nature* change? We'll leave that to the scientists and philosophers. But since, in my opinion, an investor's behavior is the greatest determinant of the success or failure of his investment strategy, can his *behavior* change?

A basic principle in Jewish thought is the concept that within each person there is a constant struggle taking place between the mind and the heart.

The heart and mind are pulling in opposite directions. The heart is only interested in obtaining what it is attracted to: what tastes good, feels good, looks good, and is enjoyable and pleasurable. The heart takes nothing else whatsoever into consideration.

The brain says, "Wait a moment. Let me examine this. Is it good? Is it bad? Is it profitable? What will the results be?" The brain takes *everything* into account.

Because the mind and heart will be pulling in opposite directions, the most fortunate person is the one who disciplines his mind to control his heart so that his decisions will be based on sound, intellectual reasoning rather than emotions. Achieving this is challenging and requires constant intellectual reinforcement.

There are many biblical sources which express and corroborate this concept. Let us mention a few:

1) In *Pirkei Avos*[15] it is written, "*Aizeh hu gibor?* – Who is strong? – i.e., how would we truly describe a mighty person?" The answer is: "*Hakoveish es yitzro* – One who is capable of conquering his impulses."

   "*SheNe'emar* – As it is written," and here the *Mishnah* quotes a verse from *Mishlei* (*Proverbs*) 16.32:

   "*Tov erech apayim migibor* – A person who is slow to anger is better than a mighty person who is physically strong";

   "*U'moshel b'rucho* – And a person who is a master of his passions is better than *mi'locheid ir* – a person who conquers an entire city."

   The truly strong person is not the one with physical powers, but he who is able to control his heart, his impulses, and his desires.

2) In the Book of *Tanya*, written by the first Rebbe of Chabad, Rabbi Shneur Zalman of Liadi,[16] the author states that G-d created human nature such that "*Moach shalit al halev* – the mind rules over the heart." The natural state of every person is that the brain is capable of ruling over the heart.

   A person might experience a strong, almost irresistible, impulse due to the pleasure he imagines he would have were he to attain the object of his desire. Nevertheless, if he recognizes and decides in

---
15. *Ethics of the Fathers* 4:1.
16. Also known to all as the Alter Rebbe.

his mind that this is something he should not do, then he has the power to control his heart's desire.

In fact, a follower of the Alter Rebbe related a story from his own life, demonstrating how this principle of the mind controlling the heart literally saved his life.

In the early 1800s, during the war between France and Russia, the Alter Rebbe believed it would be in the Jewish people's better interest if the Czar, as opposed to Napoleon, would win the war. He therefore prayed for the Czar's victory, and, in addition, did whatever he could to aid the Czar's cause. He even appointed one of his followers, Reb Moshe Meisels, to act as a spy for Russia to aid the Czar's war effort.

Reb Moshe lived in a city located between Russia and France and knew both languages. When the French Army needed French-Russian interpreters, Reb Moshe offered his services and was hired. The French never suspected that this chassid could understand more than the work they gave him to translate, so they spoke about their plans in front of him openly. Reb Moshe then passed along the information to a messenger who relayed it to the general of the Russian Army.

On a few occasions, the French were shocked that their "fail-proof" battle plans had failed. They came to the conclusion that a spy must be operating among them in the highest ranks, but although they accused many different army men, they were unable to ascertain the spy's identity.

One day, the generals were sitting in their office making plans, and at the other end of the office, Reb Moshe Meisels was working on a translation of a certain document he had been given. All of a sudden, the doors flew open and Napoleon himself entered. He scanned the room and saw the chassid working there. Napoleon screamed out, "What are you doing here?!" He then pointed his finger at him and shouted, "YOU are the spy!" As soon as these words were out of his mouth, Napoleon placed his hand on Reb Moshe's chest, over his heart, to see how fast the chassid's heart was racing. This would indicate whether or not he was actually the spy they were looking for.

We can certainly understand that anyone who would be accused of spying, even if he were totally innocent, would have a racing heart if Napoleon himself were standing before him and accusing him. Imagine the heartbeat of the person who was actually the spy!

The chassid later explained that the training he had received from his Rebbe – that the mind should always control the heart – gave him the discipline to be in complete mastery of his heart during those fateful moments to such an extent that his heart was beating normally!

When Napoleon realized that Reb Moshe's heart was beating at a regular rate, he waved his hand and said, "Impossible! This person could not be the spy." Thus, this chassidic teaching actually saved Reb Moshe's life.

3) The Talmud brings the following phrase promoting the same theme: *"Hareshoyim b'reshus libam, hatzaddikim libam b'reshusam* – The difference between the righteous and those who live a life of evil is that a righteous person is in control of his heart, whereas a wicked person is actually controlled by his heart." (*Bereishis Rabbah* 34:11)

4) Regarding the desire for money, the Torah also states that a judge who has accepted a bribe is no longer considered trustworthy (see *Devarim* 16:19). And the Torah explains: *"Hashochad yaavor einei chachamim* – When a person accepts a bribe, his eyes are blinded;

even the wisest people feel a compulsion to do anything that will help them earn the money they were given or promised."

After one has accepted a bribe, his mind can no longer evaluate the facts with the proper perspective – in other words, his heart is controlling his mind.

5) Another relevant Torah passage is: *"Al kol fesha'im tikaseh ahavah* – Love hides all faults." (*Mishlei* 10:12) Normally when we look at another person or situation, we can see his (or its) faults. But if we truly have a strong desire, love, and passion for the person or thing, suddenly all the flaws are concealed from us and we cease to see anything wrong. The reason for this is that the heart is overpowering the mind. If a person lives a life in which his mind controls his heart, he will not be blinded.

6) A similar thought appears in the Talmud (*Tamid* 32a): *"Eizehu chacham? Haro'eh es hanolad* – Who is considered truly wise? The person who sees the outcome of his actions." Ordinarily, people make judgments based on immediate gratification and/or pleasure. A wise person looks ahead to the outcome.

There are occasions when, on the surface, a venture may appear to result in incredible and immediate profits, or to provide wonderful benefit, but the wise person will look ahead and see that ultimately, the risk is too great and could result in a greater loss than the promised gain. He uses his mind to control his heart to do what is right and sound, and does not succumb to that which appears temporarily beneficial.

It is a lifetime challenge to achieve the state in which the mind controls the heart. Since fear and greed, or panic and euphoria often determine an investor's behavior, education and counsel can help alleviate the mistakes that result from following one's own emotional or psychological disposition. On some level, these feelings will most likely remain, but at least they will not cause one to act impulsively.

Sammy and the Middle East Crisis

I was about to respond to Sammy, but suddenly I was overcome with fatigue; the argument we were having had begun to wear me down. I did not understand his unwillingness to accept, or even hear, my advice. I knew, as did Sammy, that there are many stockbrokers who would gladly take his orders and execute them without question. Instead of continuing the discussion with him, I was tempted to refer him to another broker and wish him luck.

(As we were talking, I experienced a flashback to my tax client Jacob. While preparing his tax return I noticed that he purchased tax-exempt municipal bonds. Jacob's tax bracket was zero. He paid no income tax. I asked him why he purchased these bonds when he could have purchased taxable bonds paying a higher return and still pay no income tax. He responded that he heard an advertisement on the radio for the municipal bonds, called the number, and placed his order. The broker never asked him if the investment was appropriate for him.)

When I first entered the financial planning field, I enjoyed verbal sparring with others, trying to convince them of the appropriateness of my strategy. Debating was part of my childhood: as we sat around the table at dinner time, my brothers would debate any topic. One of us would always play "devil's advocate" just for the sake of it.

Of late, however, I have noticed that people rarely change their minds as a result of an argument. I can attempt to educate people regarding the advantages of a sound strategy, but arguing is a waste of time.

Listening to Sammy, I realized that he was prepared to continue our verbal battle. Rather than continue, I said, "It seems to me that we are wasting our time debating this. You approached me for my opinion on a subject that is within my area of expertise; a subject that I study daily by reading professional literature and staying abreast of the latest developments and regulations by attending conferences and seminars.

"Following our meeting and discovery session, when I came to understand your financial needs, I recommended a strategy that was appropriate for your situation. It is possible that in the future I may change my recommendation as your situation changes, but presently, my recommendation stands. You are free to accept or reject it. But why are you trying to convince me that your take on what's best for your financial needs is the best way to go?"

How did this all start? I received a call from Sammy earlier that day. He had spent the weekend watching the developments in Egypt and concluded that after law and order breaks down in Egypt, the country will collapse and there will be a domino effect on Jordan, Syria, Saudi Arabia and the entire Middle East. Oil will stop flowing to the West and the entire world will be plunged into chaos, which may end civilization as we know it.

Sammy's conclusion was to liquidate his entire portfolio and convert it to cash.

My advice was to "review every year historically and see similar scenarios that never materialized."

Sammy responded, "I would rather be safe."

"What if the dollar collapses?" I asked. "That is, what if the U.S. government goes bankrupt? How safe is the cash?"

Sammy insisted: "For now, sell everything and put it into cash. Within the next few days I will decide what to do next."

Per his instructions, I liquidated the portfolio.

Then, that very day, the following happened:[17]

Tuesday	Open	Closed	Change	
S&P 500	1,289.14	1,307.59	up 18.45	1.43%
DOW	11,892.50	12,040.16	up 147.66	1.24%

On Wednesday, the following day, the headline in the Wall Street Journal[18] read: "STOCKS HIT POST-CRISIS HIGH."

And now, the rest of the story.

Sammy repurchased his investments a few weeks later, when, as he put it, "things calmed down," but at a higher price. But selling an investment is a taxable event, and his actions resulted in a substantial tax on the sale, which would have been avoided had he done nothing!

A few days later, I called Sammy and disengaged as his financial advisor. I had done all I could to help him and could see that his approach to investing differed from mine. Perhaps what he really wanted was a sparring partner, not a financial advisor.

How to Buy Mutual Funds

As he passed by the house of a local peasant, the prince noticed an extraordinary sight. There were many archery targets in the yard, and on each target, every arrow was located precisely in the bull's-

---

17. See www.google.com/finance and https://finance.yahoo.com.
18. February 2, 2011.

eye. The prince dismounted from his horse and stepped closer to marvel at this phenomenon. He could not contain himself; he had never seen such accurate shooting. The prince requested that this peasant be brought before him.

When the trembling peasant appeared before the prince, the prince asked him, "How did you perfect your shooting? I, too, am a master archer but there are occasions when I miss the target. Every one of your arrows is precisely on the bull's-eye!"

The peasant, now a bit more relaxed, answered the prince honestly: "The difference between us is very simple. You first draw the target with the bull's-eye in the center and then attempt to hit it whereas I do the opposite. First I shoot the arrows and only then do I draw circles around them and make sure the arrow is at the center. This way my arrows are always on the bull's-eye."

At a family dinner at the beginning of the year 2000, a relative proudly announced that he had invested in a mutual fund "that increases in value 200% annually." When I questioned him, he told me that the fund had risen 211% in value in the past year. "When did you buy the fund?" I asked. "Last week," he answered, just as I had anticipated. Buying a fund that "increases 200% annually" makes for great conversation, but how did my relative do financially? During 2000, the fund lost 34% of its value and continued its negative streak, losing 40% and 41% in 2001 and 2002 respectively. By 2003, when the fund increased in value by 47%, my relative was no longer invested in the fund. He had bailed out at the end of 2002, unable to tolerate any more losses.

Everyone wants to invest in the best-performing fund or asset class. But investing in last year's best performing fund or asset class is similar to circling a bull's-eye around the arrow.

Although numerous studies have shown that there is no significant correlation between past performance and future performance, the first – and usually the only – item most investors rely on when selecting a fund is past performance.

Obviously, past performance is the easiest to understand and the most readily available piece of information available. The problem is that past performance is of little use in identifying funds or managers who will deliver superior *future* performance.[19]

Why, then, do people emphasize past performance? There are several reasons:
1) Many investors do not realize that past performance is not a factor in predicting future value.
2) The mutual fund companies and the financial media hype past performance and, in doing so, impart the misconception that it can be used to make successful investing decisions.
3) Most investors do not have the time or resources to dig beyond the numbers. Fresh research that goes beyond past performance is time-consuming and requires experience and know-how to distinguish important information from irrelevant facts.

Is a mutual fund track record useful?
(In my opinion it does not, as detailed below.)

1) **Some mutual fund managers are simply lucky**. There are thousands of skilled professionals searching for investments that will outperform the market. It is highly unlikely that one manager will continue to outperform. And when he does,
2) **His success will result in asset growth as investors flock to his fund**. A small fund has flexibility which it loses as its assets grow. This is especially true

---

19. In my experience, there's only one accurate correlation between past performance and future performance: Managers with very bad returns will consistently report bad returns in the future.

regarding the smaller cap funds. Also, as the fund's assets grow, the fund manager may be forced to own more stocks. This may not be his preferred choice because according to a fund's prospectus, there is usually a limit as to how much of the fund it may invest in any one security. And success may result in:

3) **Manager turnover**. The manager who produced the returns may no longer be managing the fund. He may have left to join another organization or start his own firm. And if he stays,

4) **The manager's "stardom" often results** in the spreading of his activities to non-investing activities as his fund company tries to capitalize on his "stardom." It will do so by attempting to attract investors by creating new financial products and giving him marketing responsibilities to promote his fund and the company he works for.

The difficulty in predicting future performance based on track record is the basis for the conclusion that low-cost index funds are a better choice. With low-cost index funds, you may not always own the best performing fund, but in my opinion, you will probably outperform most investors who search for the "best" active manager.

(Before investing, carefully consider the fund's investment objectives, risks, charges and expenses before investing. For this and other information, contact your advisor or the fund company for a free prospectus. Read it carefully before you invest or send money.)

INDIVIDUAL STOCKS:
SERIOUS BUSINESS OR SOCIAL INVESTING?

During the spring of 2000, at the height of the bull market when the Internet bubble was particularly full of hot air, my clients Harriet and her husband Alan came to my office to have their tax returns prepared. Their investment portfolio was diversified among various mutual funds.

Suddenly Harriet asked me about a company called Cisco. Initially she couldn't pronounce it correctly, but we figured out what she meant. She said she wanted to buy it and when I asked why, she answered, "Because everybody in my office is buying it and talking about it. If everyone is doing it, I am sure that they know what they are doing. Besides, until I also invest in Cisco, I won't have anything to talk about with them. Investing in mutual funds is boring."

I tried to discourage Harriet but had a feeling that my advice would go unheeded. She wanted to buy Cisco and be part of the group. When I met with them the following year to prepare their income tax returns, she and Alan told me they had purchased 200 shares of Cisco at $72 a share, which happened to be near its peak price.[20] Within a few months, when the value of the stock lost half its value, they sold it. They were so embittered by their experience, they liquidated their entire portfolio, including their mutual funds which were doing well. They lost their faith in the market.

In a revealing article about the psychology of investing, Roger Gibson, author of the book *Asset Allocation*, writes of a conversation he had with a client regarding establishing a properly diversified portfolio. The client declared, "I would rather follow an inferior strategy that wins when my friends

---

20. See finance.yahoo.com, April 3, 2000.

are winning and loses when my friends are losing than follow a superior long-term strategy that at times results in my losing when my friends are winning." (!)

Humans are social beings, and we need a sense of belonging to a group. At cocktail parties and dinner parties the conversations often turn to discussions about the stock market and, for some, it is important to be able to join in with an anecdote about their stock holdings.

I refer to this as "social investing," and it is similar to social drinking. If you need the excitement of investing in individual stocks and enjoy entertaining your friends and relatives about your exploits, by all means, do so. Just remember: as with drinking, keep it to a sensible level. This should be considered your "play money" as opposed to the serious money that you invest in a well-diversified portfolio.

> *A sensible rule of thumb is to limit your "speculating/trading money" to 5% of your total portfolio.*

Open a special brokerage account with the amount you are willing to put aside to speculate, "play," and trade to your heart's content. In any event, do not confuse your speculating/trading activity with investing. Speculating, in fact, bears a great resemblance to gambling. If you happen to have some profitable trades, do not allow your success to go to your head, because it probably stems from luck.

Beyond this, I suggest that if you want excitement, go to a casino. You will probably have more fun and lose less money that way. You will not delude yourself into believing that you are investing. You will understand that you are gambling and will limit your losses accordingly.

In all cases, your serious money should be segregated from the money you use to speculate, and should be professionally managed.

I am not implying that nobody ever made money speculating in stocks. It's simply that in my 40 years of experience of preparing tax returns, I never had a successful speculator as a client.

Phillip may be an exception. He is a professional stock trader and consistently earns close to a million dollars annually. His beginning capital (the amount with which he starts the year) in his investment account is only $100,000. In 2013, his trading activity was close to $500,000,000. That's half a billion dollars, and his year-end brokerage tax statement that listed his sales was around 4,700 pages. He may buy 1,000 shares of Apple, Inc. for $500 a share, for a total investment of $500,000, and sell the 1,000 shares 3 minutes later. Phillip is not a typical speculator. Stock trading is a full-time job for him and he is very good at it. There is a possibility that you'll make money by speculating, but since it *is* speculative, you shouldn't "play" with the money you need for the groceries.

When to sell a stock

You decide to buy a stock. When do you sell?

Studies show that individual investors tend to hold on to their losers while selling the winners. Selling a losing position confirms that you made a mistake, but if one keeps it, the possibility remains that the stock may rebound. By refusing to sell their losers, people are foregoing other opportunities in which they might use the losses to claim a loss on their tax return to offset their taxable income and save taxes.

What about a profitable position? At what point does one take one's profits?

Within six months, at the height of the Internet bubble, one of Ken's stock holdings rose from $20,000 to about

$250,000, but Ken was reluctant to sell as this would incur a large tax bill. He no longer has that problem, as the stock tumbled during the Internet bust and is now worthless.

In 1978, Eli purchased a stock. Within two weeks, he sold it at what he considered to be a substantial $1,500 profit at the time. He ruefully told me afterwards that had he held on to the stock, his position today would be worth in excess of a million dollars.

William rarely invests in individual stocks. The three stocks in his portfolio were purchased years ago and have not moved much, but he is reluctant to sell because, as he put it, "I do not know what to do." He recently bought a winner. When the shares of the stock he purchased for $42 increased to $105, he increased his position by 50%. When I asked him what his selling strategy was, he had none. He does not know much about the fundamentals of the company whose stock he purchased, but "feels good" about it.

By owning a share of stock, you own a share in the company that issued the stock, and the value of the share is generally correlated to the value of the company. Advice on analyzing the value of a company (and the underlying shares) is beyond the scope of this book. But if you own individual stocks, you should continually ask yourself one crucial question: "If I did not own this stock, would I buy it today?"

Consider each day that you possess a stock as if you had just purchased it. There is no need to continue holding a poorly performing stock. You can sell it and have the cash available for another, potentially better, performing investment. It is unfortunate that people often continue to hold stocks that are essentially a losing venture.

Martin was one of my very few clients who made money on his own in stocks. Preparing his tax return was a chore.

Although his annual earning at his full-time job was never more than $22,000, he used to bring me over 30 1099-DIV Forms, forms that companies issue to stockholders showing their dividend income for the year. However, I never had to prepare a Schedule D, the schedule to report gains and losses on the sale of stocks, because Martin never sold a stock. Accumulating stocks was his passion. Working as a clerk in a toy store, Martin achieved his desire to be a business owner by buying shares of companies, even though he could only afford to buy the stocks in small quantities of 10 to 20 shares at a time. "I own a percentage of all these companies," he would tell me proudly. At his death at age 81, Martin's estate was valued in excess of $2 million.

Martin was an investor, not a trader! An investor invests in a company for the long term and expects to benefit from the company's long-term growth. A trader hopes for a quick gain on a rapid turnover in his stock trades. The long-term growth of a company doesn't interest him – he will not be around that long. He hopes to benefit from the daily or weekly volatility of the stock.

The greatest advantage the investor has over the trader is in the tax code. Since an investor owns stocks for the long-term, usually greater than one year, he enjoys the benefit of long-term capital gains which are taxed at a low of between zero and (currently) 23.4%. The trader who holds stocks for short periods, generally less than one year, is subject to the higher short-term capital gain rates which may reach 39%.

An important principle to remember: Your return on investment has a direct inverse relationship to your trading activity. Research shows that the more you trade, the poorer will be your return (see below).

An academic research paper by Brad M. Barber and Terrance Odean titled "Trading Is Hazardous to Your

Wealth: The Common Stock Investment Performance of Individual Investors" is summarized as follows:

> Individual investors who invest in common stocks directly incur a performance penalty for active trading.[21] Of 66,465 households with accounts at a large discount broker during 1991 to 1996, those who traded most earned an annual return of 11.4% while the market returned 17.9%.
>
> Overconfidence can explain high trading levels and the resulting poor performance of individual investors. Their central message is that "trading is hazardous to your wealth."
>
> Brad M. Barber and Terrance Odean,
"Trading Is Hazardous to Your Wealth:
The Common Investment Performance of Individual Investors,"
The Journal of Finance, vol. 55, no. 2 (2000).

> The investor's chief problem — and even his worst enemy — is likely to be himself.   – Benjamin Graham

Investing in stocks: half a transaction is not enough

At one of the financial planning conferences I attended, a highly respected portfolio manager presented his views on the economy and the future direction of the stock market. At the end of his speech, I was among several attendees who gathered around him for further discussion.

When someone asked if he had any stock recommendations, his answer was noteworthy: "Of course I cannot give you any tips," he said, "because then I would lose my edge. But even if I could, or was permitted to give you a tip on an attractive stock, I would not. The reason is that a stock transaction involves two actions: buying a stock and selling

---

21. Performance penalty means that they underperformed the market compared to those individuals who did not trade so much.

a stock. Having knowledge of only half the transaction is not enough to make you successful. I might tell you which stock to buy, and you might buy it, but I will not be around to advise you when to sell it. And if I am not available for that second step, buying it might not have been a good idea in the first place."

What an insightful statement.

Unless you know how deep the water is or the direction of the currents, do not jump into the water or you might get swallowed up in the undertow. The local swimmer who knows the water and the tides is your best guide.

Why You Should Not Invest in Individual Stocks

> *"One who wishes to become wealthy should engage in raising small animals. Small animals are goats and sheep. Since their flocks multiply rapidly, raising them is conducive to attaining wealth."* — Talmud, Pesachim 50b
>
> *In another source, the Sages of the* Talmud *say the opposite:* *"One who engages in raising small animals does not meet with success."* —Talmud, Chulin 84b

The contradiction is explained as follows: In the first case, the reference is to raising flocks on the range where people do not see them grow. However, in the second case, the reference is to raising animals in a populated area, and as such, the growth of the flock attracts attention, causing the gains to be wiped out. Why? Because when others see that it is possible to successfully raise flocks, they will also raise flocks and therefore compete, and this competition will reduce the profits for everyone.

The Talmud was written between 200 and 500 CE in an economy based on agriculture and animal farming. The Sages of the Talmud related much of their wisdom and advice in language describing the farming and raising of domestic animals.

One can more easily benefit from their profound insights by changing some of the words in their examples to today's economy and investing terms. In both cases, "small animals" could simply be changed to "small company stocks." And "not see them grow," used in the explanation of the first quote, could be changed to "undiscovered value" stocks.

Value investing is a strategy of investing in companies that trade for less than their intrinsic value and whose growth potential is not recognized (i.e., not seen) by other investors. When other investors eventually realize the growth potential of these companies, this causes an increase in their value and, for future investors, the potential gains are diminished.

There is a body of research that shows that over a long investment horizon, small company stocks have outperformed their large-cap brethren. At the same time, small company value stocks outperform all other asset classes.[22]

Jerry, a client and owner of a mid-sized manufacturing corporation, asked me to come to his office to discuss his plans for the future of the business. At 72 years old, he was ready to retire and his professional children were not interested in taking over the business. I was not surprised when he told me of his plan to sell the business. "Asher, you

---

22. Ibbotson® SBBI®, Stocks, Bonds, Bills and Inflation 1926-2013.

are my CPA. What do you think the business is worth?" he asked.

Before offering an opinion, I asked, "What do *you* think it is worth?"

"How should I know?" he answered. "I may have a general idea, but I do not know how to value a business. That is your job!"

Jerry is a self-made man. He built the business himself, and he runs it himself. He also manages his investments himself. He only invests in individual stocks; never in mutual funds.

"Jerry, I have been your accountant for over 20 years, and during that time, you have bought and sold hundreds of stocks. Each of those stocks represents a business. When you bought the stock, you obviously believed it was undervalued and that the stock price would go up. When you sold a stock, you judged it to be either fully valued or overpriced, which is why you sold it. Why not use the same methodology you used in evaluating your stocks to evaluate your business?" I asked rhetorically. His facial expression showed that he did not understand my point.

"Nobody knows your business as well as you," I continued. "You know its history, future potential, the industry and competitors, the value of the equipment and its condition. You know more about your business than anyone, including me. Why are you unable to evaluate its worth?"

"Because I am not an expert!" he answered in exasperation.

"Then how do you buy stocks?" I answered.

The reality is that most people are not investors in stocks. They may be traders or speculators, but most likely, without admitting it, they are gamblers. Even the language I heard them using attests to this: "The stock went up, so I am taking money off the table," or, "I sold part of my holding, so I am playing with house money."

How else can one explain the behavior of an otherwise rational person who blindly "invests" thousands of dollars on a hot tip or, at best, with the most superficial knowledge of the underlying investment?

If, despite the odds, you decide to trade in stocks, remember the following before you make a trade:

The stock market is an auction composed of anonymous buyers and sellers, with over 88% of trading activity done by institutions.[23] When you buy a stock, someone is selling it. Ask yourself, why is he selling? Conversely, when you sell, someone is buying. Why is he buying? Since the buyer (or seller) is anonymous, does he have information you don't have? And since it is very likely that the counterparty to the trade is an institution, keep in mind that they have vastly superior information and expertise than you do.

If you've ever visited a gambling casino, you may have observed that at the roulette table, next to the wheel, there's a monitor showing the previous twenty numbers in which the ball landed. What's the purpose of the screen? Is it supposed to have predicting power over the next turn of the wheel? Of course not. Every turn of the wheel is absolutely independent of the previous turn. Yet, gamblers worldwide look at the monitor before placing their bet and selecting the number. They believe they are making the bet on a sound, intellectual basis.

Similarly, most people only analyze a company superficially. A comment I've often heard is, "I will wait for the earnings to come out, and if they are good, I will buy the stock." True, prices generally increase after positive news, but

---

23. See statspotting.com, "NYSE Daily Volume Statistics: Who Is Trading?" May 6, 2011.

the smart money is made when one buys *before* the news becomes public. Trading on inside information is illegal. Discovering "buying opportunities" can only be accomplished through research and an understanding of the information you have uncovered.

Or perhaps you can tune in to television and follow the advice of the "gurus." You and the other millions of viewers can buy the stock "before anyone else finds out...."

"Cisco is the best managed company in the world" was Peter's response when I asked him why he just purchased 1,000 shares of that company's stock. "And what does the company do?" I asked him. There was a long pause and he finally responded by saying that "they make the plumbing for the Internet."

He had no response when I followed up with the question, "What is plumbing for the Internet?"

"Do you know what Coca-Cola does?" I asked. "Of course. They make Coke." Needless to say, the above conversation took place in 2000 and by 2001 Peter lost 70% of his investment in Cisco.

PRINCIPLE: *If you still decide to invest in individual stocks, invest only in what you know and truly understand.*

Chapter 4

RETIREMENT PLANNING

THE NEED FOR RETIREMENT PLANNING

An Introduction

The lone survivor of a shipwreck was bewildered when he made it safely to shore clinging to a wooden beam. His landing place was an unknown island in a remote area of which he had never heard.

A huge crowd was waiting for him, and as they pulled him out of the water, a cheer resounded loudly in his ears. Although he was frightened, the crowd seemed friendly and warm. They took him to a beautiful palace where he was able to refresh himself and satisfy his hunger.

The next day, a distinguished delegation of the island's elders approached him and explained his situation. The island was in a remote location and unknown to the outside world. The inhabitants preferred it that way. They were a peaceful and friendly society. But they also realized the importance of having a leader, a king. They were also concerned that the leader might become an absolute monarch and ruthless dictator, so they devised a procedure whereby they would wait for a shipwreck survivor to land on their island (which happened about once a year) and they would elect him as their king.

But there was a caveat: He could only rule for one year. Following his year of rule, he would be taken to an adjacent, uninhabitable island and left to die. During his year of reign, he would have absolute power, but it would definitely end after the year. There were no exceptions. Our survivor was offered the opportunity to become king. Refusal meant immediate death.

The survivor realized his predicament and accepted. Being an intelligent person, he ruled wisely and kindly. As king, he embarked on an important and massive project that was very dear to him.

When the year was over, the same delegation that appointed him ruler came to him and informed him that, effective immediately, his reign had come to an end. They would be transporting him to the desolate island where he would surely die within a very short time. As he had been a popular monarch, the entire nation came to see him off and many joined in the voyage to the nearby island.

As they approached it, all were shocked at the scene that met their eyes. The desolate island had become a paradise. In his wisdom, the man had used the year he ruled to prepare for the future and had transformed the island into a beautiful and hospitable place. The natives conferred and decided that because of his great wisdom and kindness, they would suspend their custom and anoint him king for life.

I heard this fable when I was around nine years old, and it is a perfect metaphor for retirement planning. Regardless of the way you envision your "golden years," proper planning is essential. Unfortunately, most Americans are woefully unprepared both mentally and financially.[1]

I experienced a most eye-opening example of this when I asked Michael about his retirement planning. Michael is 54 years old and married, with an annual income of $175,000 and no savings. When asked about his retirement needs, he answered impulsively, "In addition to my Social Security income of $26,000, I'll need about $15,000 a year to live; I will not need too much money when I retire." After a five-minute conversation, he realized that even $75,000 a year may not be sufficient.

---

1. Board of Governors of the Federal Reserve System, Press Release, August 7, 2014.

The subject of retirement evokes a variety of feelings in different people. Some look forward to it and consider it their rightful reward after a lifetime of hard work, while others dread it because they feel they will face full-time boredom. When questioned, most retirees advise others never to completely retire. Being occupied and maintaining a regular schedule should be of utmost importance.

Lipa transitioned into retirement. At 72 years old, he is now "officially" retired. After he stopped working full-time at 65, he accepted part-time employment. This way he was able, as he put it, "to gradually accept the reality of being unproductive in the traditional way, and find alternate activities to occupy my time such as attending adult education courses. Stopping cold-turkey in one day is the worst way to retire."

It used to be that with a shorter life expectancy, retirement was defined in terms of the relationship of the individual to the active workforce. An individual would work full-time until a certain age and then leave employment to enjoy a few years of quiet living. Today, with longer life expectancies and healthier living, this "traditional" view of retirement is no longer applicable, and retirement is drastically different from what it was in the past.

The single most important factor changing the retirement picture is the fact that we now live much longer than before; 65 today is far younger than it used to be. As a result, many of today's retirees are opting to continue working well past their traditional retirement age of 65.

Our society's prosperity is another factor in the changing face of retirement. It enables some individuals to voluntarily choose to retire early – in their 40s and 50s – or change careers to a more enjoyable occupation. Today, retirement may be defined by the activities people pursue, such as travel, returning to school, volunteer work, or engaging in one's favorite hobbies and sports.

For example, a program on National Public Radio[2] began with the phrase "seventy is the new fifty" to describe the active lifestyle and vitality of an aging generation of people who retired from their careers and found themselves with energy and ambition far beyond the rocking chair. The program, entitled "Adults Buck Conventional Wisdom to Play Musical Instruments," described an organization called the New Horizons Band that has helped establish over 100 bands and orchestras for older players in the U.S. and Canada over the past 15 years. Many of the group's members are either complete novices or have not played in decades. These days, learning to play a musical instrument "is not just for kids anymore."

So today's retirees are making many lifestyle choices in retirement which include the many financial options that go along with those choices.

Albert, an 82-year-old retiree, and his 79-year-old wife, Rose, were receiving a monthly check of $4,000 from their investment portfolio. In addition, they receive monthly income of $2,500 from Social Security and $1,000 from an annuity. Their total annual income is about $90,000. I was surprised when he called me and said, "I need to draw an additional $1,000 a month from my investment." I questioned why they couldn't manage on $90,000, particularly since he owned his home and was free of mortgage payments.

He replied that the outlay alone for medical bills, insurance, utilities and real estate taxes was about $40,000. They live a modest life, he explained, but do like to travel occasionally and see their children and grandchildren in

---

2. Broadcast on July 3, 2006.

another state. And then he made the following observation: "You know, Asher, years ago, when I heard someone had a million dollars, I was jealous. Today I feel sorry for him."

Eighty-year-old Esther is in terrible pain from a serious bout of cancer and must travel to Sloan Kettering Hospital for a weekly chemotherapy treatment. She makes the trip by taking the subway (which is five blocks from her home), a trip that involves changing trains twice and a travel time of about an hour and a half. When I suggest that she use some of her substantial investment portfolio and take a car service, she replies that the "money is for the children." She has two children: a daughter married to a very successful surgeon and a son who is a successful businessman.

Florence knows what she wants, and spending plays a major role in her pursuit of a fulfilling life. "If nothing is left to my children, that's okay. It's my money and I want to enjoy it."

Stella and Bernard raised a family of five children, lived a simple life, and accumulated a nest egg that should provide for a comfortable lifestyle. Now that they are retired, they wish to provide financial assistance to their struggling grandchildren. Meeting them at my office, I was touched to see how happy and relieved they were when I helped them develop a plan that realized both of their objectives: a comfortable retirement and the means to help their grandchildren.

That being said, the new face of retirement, with all its possibilities, does not preclude other concerns associated with retirement, such as health issues and the need to provide a steady source of income.

The following chapters will discuss the two most important phases of your financial life:

Accumulation – saving and investing during your working period.

Distributions in Retirement – spending and investing during retirement.

Accumulation: Paying Yourself First

You owe money to a quiet but demanding creditor with a distant due date. He will not hound you for payment. How you pay him is up to you. You can satisfy your obligation by making small monthly payments over a long period of time, or wait and make a few substantial payments as you get closer to the due date. In the short term, he is very compassionate and understanding. If you can't pay him because of other expenses or even if you choose to ignore him, he'll understand. And on the due date, if you still can't pay, your debt will be forgiven. He is not the type of creditor who gets physical if you don't pay him, but later in life he'll make sure you have a most miserable existence. Your *retirement nest egg* is that most demanding creditor.

You know it's coming. You can even approximate the due date, so what can be more important than acting now to ensure a comfortable retirement? Yes, you have current pressing needs and obligations. With your income, you are stretched to the limit and retirement is far in the future. Why worry now?

On his 41st birthday, Mike called to remind me of the discussion we had when we first met. He was 26 years old and I asked him how he is financing his retirement. I remember the puzzled look in his eyes, and how he told me that he thought I was from another planet. Why would I even bring up the subject of retirement? In fact, he now confided that that question caused him to reconsider his decision to retain me as his financial advisor and accountant.

With maturity and a growing family, his perspective changed. Retirement is still years off, but it is on the horizon or, as he put it, "on my radar screen." Fortunately, he took my "old-fashioned" advice and has been funding his retirement plan for many years.

From the following example, you can see just how beneficial it is to start saving early, assuming you will get a 7% return on your investment.

A 20-year-old who wants to be a millionaire at age 65 would need to save and invest $5,000 per year for 15 years. His total investment of $75,000 would grow to $1,023,394.

If he waited until he is 30 years old to save and invest, he would need to invest $10,834 for 30 years. His total investment would be $325,022 and would grow to the same $1,023,394.

That's the power of starting early and letting the compounding effect of your return on investment work for you.

The idea that you should pay yourself first is not new. I have been using it with my clients for years and have witnessed the results. It means that when you pay your monthly bills – rent, telephone, electric, insurance, credit cards, etc. – there's one additional bill: it's from the [Your Name] Retirement Account. As the most important bill, it gets paid first.

Always!

There are always excuses to put off your monthly retirement fund payment, and besides, no one is threatening to shut off a utility if you don't pay. When you have to write the check to deposit into your retirement account, very often you simply don't.

As an accountant, my clients include employees and self-employed individuals. When self-employed individuals present me with their Form 1099-MISC (showing how much they earned), my first question is whether they made their quarterly estimated payments. The difference between an employee and someone who is self-employed is that when the employee receives his paycheck, all his taxes are *automatically* withheld by his employer and submitted to the government. The self-employed individuals receive gross payments for their services and are responsible to pay estimated quarterly taxes. Too often, as in the case above, the estimated taxes are not made, subjecting the client to penalties and interest charges.

An employee's net paycheck reflects deductions for federal income withholding taxes (up to 35%), Social Security taxes and Medicare, state and local taxes and disability and unemployment insurance. The employer is legally obligated to withhold those taxes. It could be that a worker earning $50,000 annually may bring home only $35,000 after taxes. What would happen if the worker received his $50,000 in full and by April 15 had to come up with the $15,000 in taxes? The government reckoned that people would not budget themselves and be able to pay taxes in one lump sum. For the self-employed, the government is willing to wait three months for the estimated quarterly payments, but not a whole year.

If the government wants (and gets) its share of your hard-earned income from your weekly or bi-weekly paycheck, why can't you do the same with monthly payments into your retirement accounts?

I've also noticed that when withholding income tax rates increase and the worker's net take-home pay decreases, spending is adjusted and the impact on the family's lifestyle is barely felt.

So the "pay yourself first" system requires you to "tax" yourself by submitting the amount needed to reach your retirement funding goal into your retirement account. The catch is that this "tax" must be paid on your own.

When money is saved and invested, you don't spend it

Gary is self-employed and earns different amounts every month ranging from $15,000 to $20,000. But somehow, at the end of every month, he and his wife manage to spend all their money. If he makes $15,000, they'll spend $15,000, and if he makes $20,000, they'll spend $20,000.

They started an automatic monthly investment plan that withdraws $300 from their personal checking account and invests it in a mutual fund. The only thing they have left at the end of the month is the $300 a month they set aside as a "forced" savings. If they didn't put that away, they would have spent that, too.

For the first time, Gary and his wife are actually saving money, and watching the money accumulate has had an exhilarating effect on them. Upon reviewing their account after one year, Gary increased his investment to $450 a month. He does not feel deprived nor did his lifestyle change. As he put it, "If I don't have it, I don't spend it. And honestly, I don't know where we spent the money before. It was probably on nonsense anyway." At least now he's got something to show for it.

It's never too early (or late) to start.

Distribution in Retirement and the 4% Rule

A Goal of Maintaining Financial Independence and Dignity in Retirement

Will you outlive your money or will your money outlive you? "I never want to run out of money" is the answer most retirees and pre-retirees give when I ask what their most important fear in facing retirement is. It usually follows, "I never want to turn to my children for money."

Investing consists of two phases: an accumulation phase and a withdrawal phase. During the accumulation phase, we generally invest for a specific goal. With this goal in mind – such as buying a house or a car, or setting aside money for a child's wedding – the investor knows he must save for a number of years in order to accumulate a specific amount of money. Retirement, of course, entails a goal as well. The main difference is that retirement planning involves several additional issues which are very difficult to predict:

> **Longevity:** How long will you live? Hopefully, retirement will be long-term and last 20 or 30-plus years.
>
> **Interest Rate Risks**: Will interest rates be high or low during the next five, ten or twenty years?
>
> **Market risks:** How will the stock market perform during the next five, ten or twenty years?
>
> **Inflation:** If you are spending $50,000 a year today and wish to maintain your lifestyle in retirement, and if inflation averages 3% per year, you might need over $100,000 per year 25 years from now. If you are 60 today, then by the time you reach the age

of 80 or 90, your cost of living will double or triple.

Until recently, little research was done on retirement planning because people were focused on accumulation, saving money, and nurturing its growth for the future. Today, as the baby boomer generation – 70 million strong – faces retirement, there is a great deal of research on the withdrawal phase of personal financial planning.

Furthermore, recent developments in this area have resulted in several new planning methodologies. These new methodologies allow people to do a far better job in planning for retirement – as well as managing the accumulation and distribution phases of investing – than they did in the past. My professional advisory focus has expanded to include the withdrawal phase of investing in more detail. After researching this matter, which is an ongoing area of study, I decided to plan my own financial future using the information I learned, and I advise my clients accordingly.

The year 1994 saw the publication of two very influential and original papers in the field. In William Bengen's research paper called "Determining Withdrawal Rates Using Historical Data" and published in the *Journal of Financial Planning*, the author included the historical stock market value returns from three of the worst periods in U.S. history and their impact on retirement portfolios during the withdrawal phase in retirement. The value of his research lies in his evaluation of both the best and worst times historically. The three worst periods that he analyzed were 1930-1932, 1937-1941, and 1973-1974.

Bengen reached three conclusions as a result of his research. His first conclusion was that retirees should maintain a stock allocation of between 50% and 75% during retirement. A 50% minimum allocation is required in order for a portfolio to keep up with inflation, but should not exceed a 75% maximum allocation to equities in order to keep the risk involved in maintaining a lifestyle at an acceptable level.

His second conclusion was that a maximum safe withdrawal rate during retirement is an inflation adjusted 4%. For example, consider a retiree with $1 million in his portfolio who expects his portfolio to fund his living expenses for the next 30 years: a 4% withdrawal rate will provide him with $40,000 the first year. The withdrawal amount will then adjust annually based on the annual inflation rate for the preceding 12 months. Inflation of 3% in the previous year will increase his annual withdrawal to $41,200. However, the actual performance of the portfolio must also be considered so that in years when the portfolio declines in value, the withdrawal amount is also re-evaluated. During the 2008-2009 period, when the markets had a temporary steep decline, I met with many clients to review their portfolios, and all agreed to reduce their withdrawals.

His third conclusion was that investors should plan for their portfolio to exist as long as their life expectancies plus five to ten years, depending on how conservative they wish to be.

In the second research paper, published by Larry Bierwirth and entitled "Investing for Retirement, Using the Past to Model the Future" (*Journal of Financial Planning*), Bierwirth claimed that it is wrong to assume that the rate of return for each year of a portfolio during retirement will be the same. Stock market returns vary every year, and interest rates paid by the bank or by bonds will vary over time. If a retiree encounters a bear market (i.e., a general decline) in stocks during the first portion of his retirement, he will probably outlive his money.

Markets are unpredictable and the order in which the portfolio increases or decreases (i.e, whether it's at the beginning or at the end of the distribution time period) is impossible to predict. This "order of returns," also called the "sequence of returns," presents a primary concern for retirees living on the income and capital of their investments.

Bierwirth argued that the sequence of returns is what really matters most for the portfolio during the distribution or retirement phase. Poor stock market returns early in the distribution phase means that the investor must withdraw smaller amounts from his portfolio in order to make it last a lifetime. High stock market returns early in the distribution phase can allow the retiree to withdraw higher annual amounts from his portfolio.

Over the years, additional research examined the 4% rule but has generally confirmed that Bengen's approach (the 4% rule) is a prudent strategy for retirement income planning.

The five years prior to retirement and the first five years in retirement are referred to as the "red zone" of retirement. During this period, the performance of the market (equities and interest rates) will have the greatest influence on the success or failure of the portfolio to provide lifetime income. Special care must be taken to evaluate the strategic allocation and withdrawals of the funds in the portfolio. It is essential that during this period, the investment strategy takes into account the impact of the possible sequence of returns and does not rely on long-term averages.

The following chapter continues to explore the crucial topic of "sequence of returns."

SEQUENCE OF RETURNS

Relying on averages can be potentially dangerous.

You are about to cross a river but you can't swim. You take comfort when told that the average depth is only four feet, but you weren't told that near the river banks, the river is one to two feet deep, while in the center it's ten feet deep.

Similarly, a person with his head in the oven and feet in the freezer may have an average temperature of 100, but he will be very uncomfortable.

Year	A Withdrawal	A Annual Return	A Ending Value	B Withdrawal	B Annual Return	B Ending Value	C Withdrawal	C Annual Return	C Ending Value
			750,000			750,000			750,000
1	(37,500)	20	862,500	(37,500)	8.4	775,500	(37,500)	-10	637,500
2	(37,500)	18	980,250	(37,500)	8.4	803,142	(37,500)	-19	478,875
3	(37,500)	21	1,148,603	(37,500)	8.4	833,106	(37,500)	-25	321,656
4	(37,500)	16	1,294,879	(37,500)	8.4	865,587	(37,500)	7	306,672
5	(37,500)	12	1,412,764	(37,500)	8.4	900,796	(37,500)	14	312,106
6	(37,500)	7	1,474,158	(37,500)	8.4	938,963	(37,500)	31	371,359
7	(37,500)	11	1,598,815	(37,500)	8.4	980,336	(37,500)	13	382,136
8	(37,500)	6	1,657,244	(37,500)	8.4	1,025,184	(37,500)	8	375,207
9	(37,500)	15	1,868,331	(37,500)	8.4	1,073,800	(37,500)	6	360,219
10	(37,500)	13	2,073,714	(37,500)	8.4	1,126,499	(37,500)	4	337,128
11	(37,500)	4	2,119,162	(37,500)	8.4	1,183,625	(37,500)	13	343,455
12	(37,500)	6	2,208,812	(37,500)	8.4	1,245,549	(37,500)	15	357,473
13	(37,500)	8	2,348,017	(37,500)	8.4	1,312,675	(37,500)	6	341,421
14	(37,500)	13	2,615,759	(37,500)	8.4	1,385,440	(37,500)	11	341,478
15	(37,500)	31	3,389,145	(37,500)	8.4	1,464,317	(37,500)	7	327,881
16	(37,500)	14	3,826,125	(37,500)	8.4	1,549,820	(37,500)	12	329,727
17	(37,500)	7	4,056,454	(37,500)	8.4	1,642,504	(37,500)	16	344,983
18	(37,500)	(25)	3,004,840	(37,500)	8.4	1,742,975	(37,500)	21	379,929
19	(37,500)	(19)	2,396,421	(37,500)	8.4	1,851,885	(37,500)	18	410,817
20	(37,500)	(10)	2,119,279	(37,500)	8.4	1,969,943	(37,500)	20	455,480
Average		8.4%			8.4%			8.4%	

Table 1 is an example of the impact of "sequence of returns" on a portfolio in the distribution phase.

Assume a portfolio of $750,000 and an annual withdrawal of 5% a year which equals $37,500. Also assume that the portfolio will earn an average of 8.40% over a 20-year retirement.

The table illustrates three scenarios in which all three average an 8.40% return over the 20-year period. The only difference is the sequence of the annual returns.

Column B shows results that assume the portfolio will earn an extremely unlikely return of exactly 8.40% every year. This improbable scenario will result in a portfolio that after 20 years has an ending balance of $1,969,943.

Columns A and C also result in an 8.40% average return, but the annual returns vary. For this illustration, the sequence of returns are reversed. In column A, the first year's return is 20% while in column C, the 20% is earned in year 20. Similarly, in column A, year 20 has a loss of 10% while in column C the 10% loss is in year 1.

Although the rate of return of all three portfolios averaged 8.40% over the twenty years, the portfolio values at year 20 are significantly different between portfolios A and C: they are $2,119,279 vs. $455,480 respectively.

Since the "sequence of returns risk" is related to the volatility of the market, you can completely eliminate it by investing the money you need to spend in retirement in an investment-grade bond portfolio. However, while reducing your exposure to equities would reduce your exposure to the sequence of return risk, it may also lower the potential growth of your portfolio return and reduce its potential to provide you with sufficient long-term income.

What can you do to mitigate the risk that the market's lucrative but more volatile returns don't ruin your retirement plans?

There are a number of approaches to reduce the sequence of return risk:

1. Determine your basic income requirements in retirement and attempt to provide for those needs with income from Social Security, a bond portfolio, and annuities.
2. Be flexible with your spending. Monitor your portfolio and adjust your spending during market declines.

3. Since the markets' returns in the first five to ten years of retirement will largely determine whether you'll outlive your money, consider reducing your exposure to equities in the first five to ten years of retirement and then gradually increase that percentage over time.
4. When initially determining your withdrawal rate, pay attention to the Cyclically-Adjusted Price Earnings or CAPE ratio (also known as the P/E 10 Ratio), popularized by Yale University professor Robert Shiller. "Market mean reversion"[3] may require low sustainable withdrawal rates during a bull market when market valuations are high and future growth is limited, and higher sustainable withdrawal rates after a bear market when market valuations are low and future returns may be higher.

THE INVESTMENT PLAN

Your investment strategy depends on a number of factors. But first remember that you are investing your long-term savings, that is, money you will not need (or have plans for) in the next five years and longer.

Before commencing a long-term financial plan, you must ensure that "emergency funds," usually three months of living expenses, have been set aside. These are funds you may need for unexpected events such as unemployment, home repair, medical emergency, etc.

---

[3]. A term that refers to stock market returns eventually moving back towards their mean or average historical returns. As such, periods of above average returns may be followed by periods of below average returns. (See more about this in the section entitled "Rebalancing to Remain on Course.")

With emergency funds accounted for, the following steps can now be taken to establish your financial plan:

1) **Determining your risk tolerance.** The questionnaire in the Appendix is a general guide that will gauge your attitude toward risk as it relates to evaluating the volatility of your portfolio. It consists basically of behavioral attitude questions. Since your behavior is the most important aspect in determining the success or failure of the plan, take your time and answer the questions very thoughtfully. There are no right or wrong answers. But keep in mind that you are completing the questionnaire *before* making the investment. Rather, try to imagine how you would respond if your money was invested and the market was volatile. Imagine a 10%-20% decline in the portfolio in actual dollar amounts. How would you react? Be realistic!

2) **Determining your risk capacity.** These are financial questions related to your need to tap assets for income or withdrawals, the time horizon of the goal, and what other assets are available to you. That is, to what extent would your financial goals and needs be sustained should a risky event such as a market crash occur.

3) **A key question: Which do you want to protect more, your income or your children's (if any) inheritance?** Are you willing to reduce the amount of your withdrawals from your investments — even if it impacts your lifestyle — in order to protect the future value of your estate?

4) **Examples of risk capacity.**
   a. Alan is 65 years old and retired. He has a low-risk tolerance and in a bear market would panic and sell everything immediately. To supplement his

Social Security income and pension from work, he needs $15,000 a year in income from his $1 million portfolio. Since Alan only needs to withdraw 1.5% of his portfolio yearly, he is considered to have a high capacity for risk because even if there's a substantial market crash and his portfolio declines by 50%, Alan's withdrawal rate would probably only go from 1.5% to 3%. Even if Alan can "afford" to have a growth portfolio (which would expose him to higher market volatility) should he? The answer may be different depending on whether Alan is single and childless, married, and/or has children.

5) **Do you need to withdraw funds for your current living expenses?** Set aside one to two years of the amount you'll need. If you need to withdraw $4,000 a month, keep $96,000 in a money market account and withdraw $4,000 monthly. Review the portfolio every year to determine how to replenish the money market account from the investment portfolio. The funds in the money market account will not earn much, but that's the "opportunity cost" of not having to liquidate a portion of your portfolio if there's a decline in the market and you need quick access to additional money.

6) **Allocation between fixed (bonds) and equities (stocks).** These are the two broad asset classes that are available for investments. Real estate is another asset class, but direct ownership is a business that requires hands-on work to succeed. And from what I know of many people's experience, I generally discourage people strongly from investing in real estate partnerships as minority partners/shareholders.

Based on your risk tolerance and risk capacity, you will decide on the amounts to allocate to bonds and stocks and determine whether, based on historical performance, you can pursue your goals with that allocation. It's also important to establish a benchmark for measuring the performance of the portfolio. For example, let's say your portfolio is $1 million. You set aside $80,000 (8%) to cover two years of your living expenses, and the balance is split $460,000 (46%) to bonds and $460,000 (46%) to stocks.

The benchmark you select is as follows:

Cash – 1-3-Year Treasury bonds represented by ETF SHY[4]

Bonds – Barclay U.S. Aggregate Bonds represented by ETF AGG

Stocks – S&P 500 Index represented by ETF SPY

For the year ended March 31, 2015, the benchmark return was:

	Fund	Return[5]	Allocation	Portfolio
Cash	SHY	0.91%	8%	.07%
Bonds	AGG	5.79%	46%	2.66%
Stocks	SPY	12.62%	46%	5.81%
				8.54%

---

4. EFTs (Exchange Traded Funds) are funds that track indices like the S&P 500, Dow Jones Industrial Average, etc., but trade like a stock on an exchange.

SHY – iShares 1-3-Year Treasury Bond ETF – exposure to short-term U.S. Treasury bonds. A close substitute for cash. The performance of the fund for quarter ended 3/31/2015 was 0.59, 1 year 0.91, 5 years 0.91, 10 years 2.50. Gross expense ratio is 0.15.

AGG – iShares Core U.S. Aggregate Bond ETF – core fixed-income exposure. The performance of the fund for quarter ended 3/31/2015 was 1.52, 1 year 5.79, 5 years 4.30, 10 years 4.77. Gross expense ratio is 0.08.

SPY – SPDR S&P 500 ETF – diversified exposure to 500 U.S. large company stocks. The performance of the fund for quarter ended 3/31/2015 was 0.93, 1 year 12.62, 5 years 14.29, 10 years 7.91. Gross expense ratio is 0.11.

5. www.morningstar.com.

Past performance does not guarantee future results; that the investment return and principal value of an investment will fluctuate so that an investor's shares, when redeemed, may be worth more or less than their original cost; and that current performance may be lower or higher than the performance data quoted.

You'll probably be disappointed that you only earned 8.54% compared to the 12.62% earned by the stocks. But that's the cost of your risk aversion decision, and there will be years when you'll be glad that your portfolio only decreased by a third of the stocks' decline when the markets decline.

7) **Strategic asset allocation.** Set target allocation among various asset classes (see Appendix C for an explanation of each asset class).

Eight equity diversifying funds	Four fixed-income funds
Large U.S. Stocks	U.S. Bonds
Mid-Cap U.S. Stocks	Inflation Protection Bonds
Small U.S. Stocks	Non-U.S. Bonds
Developed Non-U.S. Stocks	Cash – Money market, Bank CDs,
Emerging Non-U.S. Stocks	Short-term U.S. Treasury bonds
Real Estate	
Natural Resources	
Commodities	

These major asset classes can be divided further. For example, large U.S. stocks can be divided into value, growth or blended stocks. U.S. bonds are divided into U.S. government bonds, investment grade bonds, high-yield, short-term, intermediate-term or long-term. In addition to the asset classes listed above, Wall Street and some fund companies offer variations and innovations such as long/short, managed futures, market neutral, alternatives, etc.

My advice is to remember my initial recommendation for building a successful investment strategy: *keep it simple and boring*. "Wall Street" is essentially a large marketing machine and many fund companies market the latest fads. *After* a market decline they'll hype the bond funds. *After* the stock market had a "run up" (an increase in value) they'll promote the funds that outperformed. By following the latest investment fads, you'll always be buying *last year's* winners! Since last year's winners tend not to repeat, there's a good chance you'll be disappointed, and continuing a cycle of buying last year's winners may cause you to underperform a strategy that simply selects a fund with an appropriate benchmark and makes a commitment for a long-term investment in it, selling only when rebalancing is necessary or your goals have changed.

Now you need to "put it all together." The allocation of your money among the different asset classes should be apportioned according to your risk tolerance, risk capacity, the need for income from the portfolio, your time horizon, and any special goals.

In discussing asset allocation, the U.S. Securities and Exchange Commission writes: "Determining the appropriate asset allocation model for a financial goal is a complicated task. Basically, you're trying to pick a mix of assets that has the highest probability of meeting your goal at a level of risk you can live with."[6]

It continues: "A diversified portfolio should be diversified at two levels: *between* asset categories and *within* asset categories…. The key is to identify investments in segments of each asset category that

---

6. See www.sec.gov/investor/pubs/assetallocation.htm.

may perform differently under different market conditions."

The following is a sample portfolio. The broad allocation is 40% bonds and 60% equities. The portfolio can be further allocated:

Bonds
- Investment grade bonds — 17.5%
- Inflation protection bonds — 10.0%
- Non-U.S. bonds — 7.5%
- High-yield bonds — 5.0%

Equities
- Large U.S. stocks – Blend — 7.5%
- Large U.S. stocks – Value — 7.5%
- Mid-Cap U.S. stocks — 5.0%
- Small-Cap U.S. stocks – Blend — 4.5%
- Small-Cap U.S. stocks – Value — 4.5%
- Developed Non-U.S. stocks — 15.0%
- Emerging Non-U.S. stocks — 5.0%
- Real Estate — 6.0%
- Natural Resources — 5.0%

The above is only an illustration of a diversified portfolio. There is no single asset allocation model that is right for every financial goal. You'll be making a very personal choice and you'll need to use the one that is right for you.

8) **Passive or active.** You are now ready to select the actual investment for each asset class. Assuming you choose to implement your strategy with mutual funds, you'll need to decide between two types of mutual funds: mutual funds that are managed and those that are indexed. The former are actively

managed by an individual manager, co-managers, or a team of managers.

The index funds are passively managed, meaning that their portfolios mirror the components of a market index. For example, the well-known Vanguard 500 Index Fund is invested in the 500 stocks of Standard & Poor's 500 Index on a market capitalization basis.

Some investors are committed to actively managed mutual funds. Others are likewise committed to owning only funds that simply follow an index. The actively managed crowd seeks to outperform the market, while the indexers are satisfied with market returns.

The debate over "passive" versus "active" investing has been going on for about 40 years, and in academic research studies the majority of active fund managers came up short: In most major categories of equity mutual funds, investors would have been better off just owning the market as a whole instead of trying to beat it.[7]

My investment strategy favors index investing, but for some asset classes I use active managers. Does it have to be an either/or decision? The following are some reasons why I find index investing compelling:

a. Simplicity. Broad-based market index funds make asset allocation and diversification easy.

b. Low portfolio turnover means lower costs and fewer tax consequences.

c. Indexing is considerably less expensive than active management.

---

7. See www.financial-planning.com, "Active vs. Passive Investing: Which Wins?" Paula Vasan, September 25, 2013.

d. Passive indexing eliminates any concern of human judgment error. With an index you know what you own.
e. As an actively managed fund becomes larger, its size can adversely affect performance. Portfolio size is of no concern when dealing with passive index funds because it simply tries to duplicate the underlying index.
f. Performance. Index funds have outperformed the majority of funds over a variety of periods.[8]

9) **Monitoring and rebalancing.** The cliché is that the only thing we can be sure of when it comes to the market is that it will fluctuate. So it is important to monitor your portfolio at a pre-set interval, preferably quarterly (unless a major upheaval occurs); more often would be counterproductive. The reason, as explained earlier in the book, is that it is important to rebalance the portfolio to pursue risk management and maintain long-term investing goals. So when should you rebalance?

Let's say, for example, your selected portfolio is 40% bonds and 60% equities. A month later you notice that bonds are now 41% and equities are 59%. Should you rebalance? Not recommended. If you did, you would incur excessive transaction costs from buying and selling, and gains would result in short-term tax liabilities that can be substantially greater than long-term capital gain. Capital gains are considered long term when the investment is held for longer than one year.

Preferably, the portfolio should be rebalanced on a regular interval, such as every six or twelve months.

---

8. S&P Indices Versus Active Funds (SPIVA), U.S. Scorecard, Aye M. Soe, CFA, Year-end 2013.

Alternatively, trigger points can be set to rebalance when the relative weight of an asset class increases or decreases more than a certain pre-set ratio. In either case, rebalancing tends to work best when done on a relatively infrequent basis and, considering tax consequences, once annually is preferable.

10) **Changes to your strategy.** Recognize that portfolios fluctuate (and sometimes the temporary declines are severe) and at times appear to be a roller-coaster ride in the short term. Even so, you should not become emotional about your portfolio and change the asset allocation. There are certain obvious times, however, when it is wise to consider changing the strategy of your portfolio because of a change that occurs in your time horizon and capacity for risk. These times include:

   a. when investment goals change;
   b. when your target retirement goal is within your reach or your income level significantly changes;
   c. when the time horizon for withdrawing funds from your portfolio changes (e.g., you've reached retirement age or have retired);
   d. when life conditions change, e.g., medical, emergencies, marriage, divorce, etc.;
   e. you realize that your tolerance for risk is not as high as you thought.

   Changes to your investment strategy should be considered carefully and should not be made in a time of duress. Professional advice at these times can be invaluable.

Managing Uncle Sam, Your Tax Partner

Financial books generally include detailed information on the latest tax regulations and advice on how to minimize your tax burden. Because I am a Certified Public Accountant, the reader might expect that this book would include a chapter on tax-saving ideas, but I believe this would be a disservice to the readers. The Internal Revenue Service Tax Code changes so frequently that it is possible that the rules will change by the time you read this chapter. For example, in the past four years the following new tax bills became law:

- Tax Increase Prevention Act of 2014.
- American Taxpayer Relief Act of 2012.
- Middle-Class Tax Relief and Job Creation Act of 2012.
- Tax Relief, Unemployment and Affordable Care Act of 2010

Furthermore, old knowledge is hard to leave behind, and new laws are easily misinterpreted or misunderstood.

The general public's lack of knowledge of the tax code is sometimes astonishing. For example, many years ago, there was a special exclusion from a "tax on the gain" when senior citizens sold their homes. That law changed in 1980. The old law was replaced with a new provision that under certain conditions, couples filing a joint tax return are exempt from income tax on the gain of no more than the first $500,000 on the sale of their home ($250,000 is the exemption for singles). In my experience, almost every senior citizen who now sells his home still believes the pre-1980 rules apply. Misinformation regarding tax laws has caused untold misery to people in a variety of other situations, including the following cases.

Jason expected a large refund on his 2010 income tax return. He knew about the $8,000 credit for purchasers of first-time homes, publicized widely by the politicians, and this credit was a factor in his decision to buy a home. He was shocked when his refund was only $259. What happened to the much-ballyhooed $8,000 credit? He never heard that this credit was phased out for couples earning over $150,000, and Jason's income was $156,000.

Dan left my office close to tears. He had been laid off during that year and had struggled to make ends meet by subsisting on unemployment checks and withdrawals from his savings. With six children, this was an enormous challenge. The silver lining in the cloud was knowing that his low income would qualify him for a total of $9,000 Earned Income Credits (EIC) upon receiving his federal and state income tax returns.

With his income level and dependents, Dan definitely would have qualified for the credit, except for this disqualifier: If one's investment income (interest, dividends and capital gains) is greater than $3,000, no credit is granted. Dan's interest and dividends for the year were $3,147. The excess of $147 disqualified him from the credit and "cost" him $9,000.

Regardless of income level, everyone needs to consult with his or her tax advisor whenever life-changing events occur (divorce, unemployment, new employment, business, death, or a birth) or when one is contemplating major financial decisions.

Jason could have asked his employer to delay paying his salary for work done in the last two weeks of December, thereby reducing his income to below the $150,000 threshold. Dan could have reviewed his investment portfolio and sold a mutual fund that had an unrealized loss of $300, reducing his investment income to below the $3,000 threshold. But neither man ever thought to seek advice.

Always remember: The government is your partner, but it is the *preferred* partner, with the rules skewed in its favor. When you win, it splits the gains with you. When you have losses, they are yours alone.

Joe was not prepared when disaster struck. He entered the stock market Internet boom in early 1999 and was lucky to sell a substantial portion of his portfolio at the beginning of 2000, right before the market peaked. By April 2000, he had realized capital gains of almost $1.5 million and an income tax liability of about $450,000. Rather than set aside the money for income taxes, he reinvested his proceeds into other "dot com" stocks. By April 2001, as the Internet bubble burst, Joe was broke. Since he incurred his losses in 2001, he could not offset them against his year 2000 gains.

By April 15, 2001, when his 2000 tax return was due, his only option was to enter into an installment payment agreement (including penalties and interest) with the Internal Revenue Service. While gains are fully taxable in the year earned, losses on investments can only be deducted a maximum of $3,000 per year, so Joe would have a $3,000 deduction for the next 500 years! He could also use the losses to offset capital gains in the future. But right now Joe is broke, with no prospects for investments in the foreseeable future.

Henry has been in the restaurant business for many years. When I first met him, he had already built, operated and sold over twenty restaurants, starting in 1964 when he sold food out of a truck to the workers building the World's Fair in Queens.

Henry was a restaurant "turnaround" specialist. He would buy a failing restaurant, or build a restaurant, operate it for a year or two, then sell it for a substantial profit. He had been doing this for many years and Henry was nothing if not thorough, which I discovered when I became his accountant. Before Henry made any deal to buy or sell a restaurant, he would call me, as he would call his attorney and his other advisors, to discuss the transaction; in my case, the tax aspects.

I recall one particular time that he was considering a deal and called me for advice. "Henry," I asked, "why are you calling me? You know the ins and outs of starting a restaurant probably better than I do; you've gone through this so many times, you even know all about the tax issues, so why are you asking me?"

His answer was very simple: "Just in case I missed something. You're my CPA, my accountant. The tax laws change so frequently that you might be aware of some change in the law, however minute, that might have a great impact on this transaction. I'm calling you, I'm calling my attorney, and I'm calling all my other advisors in case I missed something."

Here is a very seasoned businessman who understands the importance of professional advice from knowledgeable and experienced professionals. Though his knowledge of the restaurant industry exceeds even that of his advisors, he was still concerned about the possibility that he might overlook some minute detail that could make a difference and affect his deal. He knew everything about the restaurant business, but did he know everything about tax laws and any changes made in the law since his last deal?

That's why he retained me and other professionals. And he would always call and ask; a smart businessman using his advisors wisely.

Chapter 5

CLOSING THOUGHTS

THE GOOD THAT FINANCIAL ADVISORS DO

> *[The job of a financial advisor should be to] provide custom-designed knowledge and wisdom in a world of overwhelming and confusing information.* — Dan Sullivan, strategic coach

The following story was told to me by Jeffrey Frieder (a friend, CPA and advisor), and illustrates the enormous value of a financial advisor's impact on one's investment issues.

During the stock market "meltdown" in 2008-2009, a client's investment portfolio declined from $1,300,000 to $1,100,000 and the client called him to express her concern. He could discern the fear in her voice and tried to calm her by reminding her of her long-term goals and explaining the market's volatility, which at times can be severe. He advised her to stay the course. The strategy on which they agreed was to monitor the portfolio, and if the value would decline to $950,000, they would consider liquidating the portfolio.

Subsequently, the portfolio's value declined to $915,000. Jeffrey called the client and said that although he strongly disagreed with selling, he was ready to honor their agreement and sell. The client told him she would discuss the matter with her husband and call him the next day. When she called, she informed him of their decision to follow his advice and not sell.

In July of 2013, the client called Jeffrey and told him that she wanted to thank him. Jeffrey asked for what reason, and she said, "I want to thank you for talking us out of selling." At that time the portfolio's value was $3,100,000.

The story with Daniel was different. He was focused on the performance of his investment portfolio when he came to my office. His intention was to review each individual fund in his portfolio to determine whether they were top performers in their asset class and to make changes if necessary.

After spending about 15 minutes analyzing the portfolio, I asked him if we could stop and discuss another important matter. I prepared an analysis of the total net worth of his assets, his income, and his living expenses. He was 58 years old at the time and intended to retire at age 66. I knew his current cost of living and asked him to estimate his cost of living at retirement.

Inputting the variables into a sophisticated financial planning software, I demonstrated a cash flow projection to him, showing that his investment portfolio would be liquidated when he would turn 74; and his wife, 69. If that happened, they would be limited to living on his and his wife's Social Security benefits which were estimated at an annual total of only $38,000.

He was visibly shaken and asked how that could be. His investment portfolio was valued at $700,000. I explained to him that since he wanted to maintain a comfortable lifestyle in retirement – spending $150,000 annually and increasing his cost of living by the rate of inflation which we estimated would be 3% annually – his investments could not support such a large annual withdrawal. Even if his investments were able to generate an additional 2% to 3% annual return over the current returns (by investing more aggressively), the money would only last another two to three years, to age 76.

Actuarially, one of them was expected to live to age 90 or longer, and living on $38,000 a year was clearly unacceptable. We scheduled a follow-up meeting, and he came with his wife. This was getting serious!

After a lengthy discussion, a plan was formulated. Their combined annual income was about $200,000. They decided to reduce their spending by $3,000 a month and invest that amount in their portfolio. If possible, Daniel would continue working to age 70, when he would receive the maximum Social Security benefits, and at retirement they would now plan to spend only $125,000 a year.

The future is uncertain, but the plan, which will be reviewed annually, now projects that the money will last to age 95. Shifting the conversation from the portfolio's performance to the truly important matter of not outliving their money provided Daniel and his wife with the clarity and confidence that were crucial to their progress.

While there are many stories about those who chose not to listen to their advisor's advice and suffered the consequences, there are many more whose successful relationship with their advisor fostered the conveyance of sound advice and practical insights, assisting them on a pathway to financial independence.

A Final Thought

At a holiday dinner, I was seated next to the general manager of a group of hospitals in a foreign country. In the course of our conversation, the topic turned to the healthcare system in his and other countries as compared to the system in the United States. After a lively discussion, he concluded his remarks by saying, "It is interesting that when people give heartfelt wishes to one another, the most common sentiment they express is that of good health.

However, we know that the people on the Titanic had good health; what they needed was *luck*!"

How true. Whenever I begin a new relationship with a client, I always remind him or her that although I will always have their best interests in mind and will continually strive to do the finest possible work, another ingredient is still needed: good fortune.

In Hebrew, we call this *sayata diShmaya*, Heavenly assistance.

May good health *and* good fortune follow you all your days, and may you always be in a position to help others and to give from your G-d-given abundance.

APPENDICES

APPENDIX A

LETTING THE FOX DIVIDE THE SHEEP

Financial planning is about more than managing investments. Topics discussed with clients include estate planning, life insurance, cash flow management, education planning, retirement planning and business succession planning. It is essentially life planning.

This chapter does not involve investments per se, but in its own way, the issue discussed here is an example of a situation that can have serious repercussions on one's finances.

Patricia never expected her daughters to end up in court. Without realizing the ramifications of what she was doing, she had a will made that was unintentionally vague. When she passed away, each daughter claimed ownership of a certain item. The item had small financial value but apparently an enormous emotional attachment to each daughter. Deciding who should inherit that item delayed finalizing the distribution of the estate's other assets by over three years, cost over $50,000 in legal fees (which continue to grow), and caused an irreconcilable split in the family.

The matter of Patricia's will and the resulting family conflict reminded me of the following parable I heard during a vacation in Central America.

A wolf had just captured and killed a sheep and was ready to devour the carcass when a lion appeared at the scene. "Move over," roared the lion. "I am the king of all the animals and I should eat first. You'll get the leftovers."

"That's not fair," responded the wolf. "I worked hard to capture this meal, and I should eat first."

The lion saw the logic in the wolf's argument, but he was still the king. After a spirited argument, they agreed to let the fox, who is known as the wisest of all animals, mediate their conflict.

After each presented his argument, the shrewd fox ruled that they cut the sheep in half with each getting half. Logic prevailed and they both agreed. So the fox proceeded to cut the sheep in half, but when he cut it, he cut one side too large: the wolf's portion was bigger than the lion's; instead of 50-50 it was 60-40.

They both looked at it and the fox said, "You know what? It's really not fair that one of you should get a bigger piece. Why don't I cut off the extra 10%? That will reimburse me for my effort in this matter." They agreed and the fox cut more from the sheep's carcass and placed the piece in his domain.

This time the lion's share was larger, so the fox had to even out the pieces again. This happened a few times, and each time, the excess went to the fox. Finally, when only a small piece was left, the fox succeeded in equally cutting the remaining pieces. By then, of course, the fox had a full belly.

Who are the foxes of our society?

While on this same vacation in Central America, I was in the passenger seat of a van as we were driving through a remote village. A motorcycle that was being ridden on the dirt road on our right – with its driver and three "passengers" clinging to its two seats – suddenly veered onto the main road that we were on and cut us off.

As our driver swerved left to avoid the motorcycle and hit the brakes, the motorcycle driver lost control and directed his vehicle into the path of the van. The impact was at the van's right side where I was sitting. The windshield in front of me shattered, and all four passengers on the motorcycle flew about fifteen feet in the air.

I will never forget the moment of impact. A million thoughts raced through my mind in the next few minutes. Here we were, a bunch of "gringos" without the ability to communicate in Spanish. Would a lynch mob be coming for us?

Amazingly, a police vehicle happened to be at the site, and thankfully, even at this remote location, an ambulance was summoned and appeared within ten minutes, removing the four injured motorcycle passengers to the hospital. The ordeal the van driver and I endured for the rest of that day is not relevant to this story, but what happened next is.

According to the laws of this country, the fact that it was the motorcycle driver's fault was irrelevant. Since the van hit the motorcycle, the van driver was presumed to be guilty. Miraculously, none of the injuries were very serious. The next day, as the extent of the injuries became known, the van driver and an insurance company representative went to the hospital where they met with the injured and their family members. Within half an hour, they concluded a negotiated settlement. The injured were immediately given cash by the van driver, and they, in turn, signed a release preventing them from pressing charges. The entire proceeding was observed and approved by a representative of the Ministry of Public Health.

I watched the proceedings in astonishment as I recalled my wife's ordeal when several years prior, she was injured and required surgery. The legal matter took close to three years and the fox received his customary 33% plus expenses. The other side, of course, incurred substantial legal fees as well.

Too often, disputes that can be settled amicably end up in prolonged litigation. When emotions are high, especially in the case of an inheritance or a divorce, the need to win "on principle" has a destructive impact on the financial well-being of all the litigants.

Before your case even goes to court, between the lawyers and the judges and the delays and the time, your portion of the settlement becomes a fraction: Their belly will be full and yours will still be growling.

This chapter was included in this book with the hope that disputes, especially among family members, be settled harmoniously, and unnecessary expenses that can diminish the preservation of one's wealth be avoided.

Appendix B

Risk Profile Questionnaire

Select One Response Per Question

1. What is your investment time horizon?
   1. ___ Less than five years
   2. ___ Five to ten years
   3. ___ More than ten years

2. Understanding that investments are not guaranteed, which best describes the investment approach you would be most comfortable with in pursuing your financial goals?
   1. ___ **Conservative**: I am willing to accept modest portfolio value fluctuation with infrequent quarterly losses in exchange for the potential of more consistent average returns.
   2. ___ **Moderate**: I am willing to accept short-term portfolio value fluctuation with an occasional year of negative returns in exchange for the potential of positive returns over the long term.
   3. ___ **Aggressive**: I am willing to accept a higher degree of portfolio value fluctuation with periodic years of negative returns in exchange for the potential of higher positive returns over the long term.

3. Six months after you make a $100,000 investment, it decreases in value by $10,000 in a down-market period. Which best describes how you would feel?

1. __ Very uncomfortable. I would consider selling my investment.
2. __ Uncomfortable, yet I will stay with the investment if my financial advisor recommends it.
3. __ I would want to buy more of the investment, since this may be a good investment opportunity.

4. Is it important for you to receive money from your account on a monthly basis?
1. __ Yes, it is highly important, and it must be the same amount each month.
2. __ It is important, but the growth of my portfolio is also an important factor.
3. __ It is not important, and the growth of my portfolio is my primary goal.

5. Although past performance is no guarantee of future results, historically, stocks have provided better protection against inflation than bonds. Additionally, diversification using a portfolio of stocks or stock mutual funds also provides the potential for less volatility in returns. Given these factors, complete the following statement: "I would be comfortable if a well-diversified position in stocks or stock mutual funds represented..."
1. __ A small percentage of my portfolio (less than 50%).
2. __ A significant percentage of my portfolio (50%-80%).
3. __ A dominant percentage of my portfolio (more than 80%).

6. The table below shows four hypothetical portfolios with fictitious yearly and seven-year average annual return numbers.[1] Consider how you'd feel if you experienced these

---

[1] *The rates of return shown above are purely hypothetical and do not represent the performance of any individual investment or portfolio of investments. They are for illustrative purposes only and should not be used to predict future product*

hypothetical returns – especially the down years – in your portfolio. With which hypothetical portfolio (A to D) would you feel most comfortable (check options 0-3 in the following table)?

	Portfolio	Year 1	Year 2	Year 3	Year 4	Year 5	Year 6	Year 7	Average Annual Return
0.___	A	3%	3%	3%	3%	3%	3%	3%	3%
1.___	B	14%	-1%	20%	-5%	10%	2%	6%	6%
2.___	C	19%	-3%	26%	-13%	15%	5%	10%	7.5%
3.___	D	25%	-5%	38%	-23%	19%	7%	14%	9%

RISK PROFILE SCORE (add the numbers checked in questions 1-6):_____

Investor Profile	Risk Profile Score
☐ Conservative Income (CI)	5-7
☐ Income (I)	8-10
☐ Conservative Growth (CG)	11-13
☐ Growth (G)	14-16
☐ Maximum Growth (MG)	17-18
☐ Maximum Growth without Fixed Income (MGnF)	17-18

In addition to the Risk Profile Questionnaire above, the following are additional questions to consider in determining your risk tolerance. Review these questions yourself or with your financial advisor to determine your recommended portfolio and its mix of assets:

1. What is your age? _____   **Your spouse's age?** _____

2. If you own a home, do you have more than 30% equity?

---

performance. Specific rates of return, especially for extended time periods, will vary over time. There is also a higher degree of risk associated with investments that offer the potential for higher rates of return.

a) No
   b) Yes
   c) I don't own a home

3. **Which of the following best describes your current employment situation?**
   a) Full-time
   b) Part-time
   c) Retired
   d) Unemployed

4. **How much investing experience do you have with stocks or stock mutual funds?**
   - None ___
   - A little ___
   - A fair amount ___
   - A great deal ___

5. **How much investing experience do you have with bonds or bond mutual funds?**
   - None ___
   - A little ___
   - A fair amount ___
   - A great deal ___

6. **What is your investment goal?** (Check all that are applicable)
   - Retirement ___
   - Saving for major purchase ___
   - More current income ___
   - Other: _____

7. **How many years do you have until retirement (i.e., when you stop working)?**

- Already retired ___
- 5 to 10 years ___
- 5 years or less ___
- More than 10 years ___

8. **What do you expect to be your next major expenditure?**
    - Buying a house ___
    - Providing for retirement ___
    - Paying for children's education ___
    - Capitalizing a new business ___
    - Other: _____

9. **How many years until this expense is incurred?**
    - 5 years or less ___
    - 5 to 10 years ___
    - More than 10 years ___

10. **What are your major objectives for your investments?**
    - Current and future income ___
    - Keeping ahead of inflation ___
    - Preserving capital ___
    - Increasing returns ___
    - Building wealth for heirs ___

11. **When do you expect to use the bulk of the money you are accumulating in your investments?**
    - At any time now ___
    - In 1 to 5 years ___
    - In 6 to 10 years ___
    - In 11 to 20 years from now ___

12. **Over the next several years, what do you expect your annual household income to do?**
    - Stay about the same ___

- Decrease moderately ___
- Grow moderately ___
- Decrease substantially ___
- Grow substantially ___

13. What percentage of your gross annual income have you been able to save in recent years?
- None ___
- 1 to 5% ___
- 6 to 10% ___
- 11 to 15% ___
- More than 15% ___

14. Over the next few years, what do you expect will happen to the percentage of your income that you will save?
- Decrease substantially ___
- Decrease slightly ___
- Stay the same ___
- Increase slightly ___
- Increase substantially ___

15. I am expecting an inheritance of approximately $_____ in:
- 0 to 5 years ___
- 6 to 10 years ___
- 11 to 15 years ___
- More than 15 years ___

16. What are your return expectations for your portfolio?
   a) I don't care if my portfolio keeps pace with inflation; I just want to preserve my capital.
   b) My return should keep pace with inflation, with minimum volatility.

c) My return should be slightly more than inflation, with only moderate volatility.
d) My return should significantly exceed inflation, even if this could mean significant volatility.

17. **How large of a temporary decline in your portfolio are you willing to accept before changing your investment strategy (assuming that you start with $100,000)?**
    - A 10% decline (portfolio value is now $90,000) ___
    - A 15% decline (portfolio value is now $85,000) ___
    - A 20% decline (portfolio value is now $80,000) ___
    - A 25% decline (portfolio value is now $75,000) ___
    - A 50% decline (portfolio value is now $50,000) ___

18. **By what percentage do you expect your portfolio to grow annually over the long term (10+ years)?**
    - 6-8% ___
    - 8-10% ___
    - 10-12% ___
    - 12-14% ___
    - 14-16% ___
    - More than 16% ___

It is your responsibility to notify your Advisory Consultant if you have any changes to your financial situation that could affect the way your portfolio is managed.

Appendix C

Definitions

Large-cap – abbreviation of the term "large market capitalization." It refers to the largest companies by market capitalization. Market capitalization is the number of the company's outstanding shares multiplied by the price per share. These are generally the largest U.S. corporations, each with a capitalization value of more than $10 billion and together comprise about 75% of the total market capitalization in the United States.

Small-cap – refers to the smallest companies with a market capitalization of between $300 million and $2 billion. Small-cap companies generally represent about 10% of the total equity market in the United States. The value of securities of smaller issuers may be more volatile than those of larger issuers.

Fixed income – securities that pay a specific interest rate, such as bonds, a money market instrument, etc. Fixed-income investment yield, share price, and total return change daily and are based on changes in interest rates, market conditions, other economic and political news, and the quality and maturity of its investments. In general, bond prices rise when interest rates fall, and vice versa. This correlation is usually more pronounced for longer-term securities.

International equity – investments in companies located outside the United States. International investing involves a special risk not present with domestic investments due to factors such as increased volatility, political and economic uncertainties, currency fluctuations and differences in auditing and other financial standards.

Real Estate – includes investments in direct ownership of rental properties or indirectly through real estate mutual funds or exchange traded funds (ETFs). Changes in real estate values, increases in interest rates, or economic downturns can have a significant negative effect on the real estate industry.

Alternatives – refer to mutual funds or ETFs which employ a non-traditional investment approach. A traditional investment approach is typically restricted to a specific mandate; for example, a large-cap U.S. equity manager is typically restricted to owning primarily large-cap U.S. equities. A non-traditional – alternative – approach typically targets a specific return, or a specified level of portfolio risk, and may invest in multiple asset classes without a mandated portfolio mix. These strategies may use derivatives or leverage, and may be less transparent than a traditional approach. These strategies do not offer any guarantee of investment performance, are subject to risk loss, and typically cannot be compared to traditional broad-market benchmarks.

Commodities – investments that provide direct holdings in commodities such as gold, silver, oil, agricultural products, etc. Commodity mutual funds and ETFs provide the investor with an opportunity to invest in commodities without taking actual possession. For example, rather than buying gold directly, you can invest in a mutual fund that invests exclusively in gold. There are mutual funds and ETFs that invest in a single commodity and others that invest in a basket of commodities, giving you exposure to multiple commodities. Investing in commodities may provide risk diversification in a portfolio, especially during periods of high inflation.

S&P – Standard & Poor's is a corporation that rates stocks and corporate and municipal bonds according to risk profiles. The S&P 500 is an index of 500 major, large-cap U.S. corporations. You cannot invest directly in an index.

DIJA – Dow Jones Industrial Average is unmanaged and measures broad market performance. It is not possible to invest directly in an index.

Unless sourced, the rates of return shown in this book are purely hypothetical and do not represent the performance of any individual investment or portfolio of investments. They are for illustrative purposes only and should not be used to predict future product performance. Specific rates of return, especially for extended time periods, will vary over time. There is also a higher degree of risk associated with investments that offer the potential for higher rates of return. You should consult with your representative before making any investment decisions.

Asset allocation and diversification do not assure or guarantee better performance and cannot eliminate the risk of investment losses.

APPENDIX D

RECOMMENDED READING

The Richest Man in Babylon, George S. Classon
> Written in the 1920s, it remains one of the most important books on personal finance. A required reading for my children, and eventually my grandchildren.

Simple Wealth, Inevitable Wealth, Nick Murray
> The author is one of the industry's premier speakers. A simple, clear, and extremely readable book. Describes investor behavior necessary to accumulate wealth.

Winning the Loser's Game, Charles Ellis
> A practical approach to wise investing.

Stocks for the Long Run, Jeremy J. Siegel
> An excellent book about investing in stocks and why stocks should be the preferred choice for the long-term investor.

Why Smart People Make Big Money Mistakes and How to Correct Them, Gary Belsky
> A fascinating and practical manual: Looking at the ways we spend, save, borrow, invest, and waste money.

The Art of Thinking Clearly, Rolf Dobelli
> Interesting reading for anyone with important decisions to make.

When Genius Failed, Roger Lowenstein

A fascinating tale of world-class greed, and the catastrophic losses that threatened the stability of the financial system itself. *(A testament to keeping things simple and boring.)*

Man's Search for Meaning, Viktor E. Frankl

Inspiring book to discover meaning in the very act of living, with lessons for spiritual survival.

About the Author

Asher Lieblich[1] is the principal in a New York City-based Certified Public Accounting firm as well as a financial services firm, Lieblich Financial Services, since 1976. His firm works with clients throughout the world and is focused on small to mid-sized businesses, real estate investment projects, professional firms and individuals committed to becoming financially independent. Asher has been ranked among the most successful investment advisors of a nationwide investment service firm and has held this distinction since 2006.[2]

Asher graduated from Brooklyn College with a Bachelor's degree in accounting and proceeded to earn a Master of Business Administration (MBA) in taxation from Long Island University. He is a Certified Public Accountant (CPA) and a member of the American Institute of Certified Public Accountants and the New York State Society of

---

1. Asher Lieblich is an advisor with H.D. Vest. The views and opinions presented in this book are those of Asher Lieblich and not of H.D. Vest Financial Services® or its subsidiaries. All investment-related information in this book is for informational purposes only and does not constitute a solicitation or offer to sell securities or insurance services. Securities offered through H.D. Vest Investment Services^{SM}, Member: SIPC; Advisory Services offered through H.D. Vest Advisory Services^{SM}, 6333 North State Highway 161, Fourth Floor, Irving, TX 75038, 972-870-6000.

    Investments and Insurance Products are not insured by the FDIC or any federal government agency; are not deposits of, or guaranteed by, the bank or any bank affiliate; and may lose value.

    Lieblich Financial Services is not a registered broker/dealer or independent investment advisory firm.

2. Asher has been a premium advisor of HD Vest Investment Services^{SM} since 2006. Premium advisor status is based on advisors rolling gross recorded on April 30th each year and accounts for 10-15% of HD Vest Advisors.*

    Source: HD Vest Financial Services – (972) 870-6000.

Certified Public Accountants. Asher is also a Certified Financial Planner™ (CFP®). He holds a Series 7 general securities license and has been a registered representative and advisor representative with H.D. Vest Investment Services℠ and H.D. Advisory Services℠ since 1990.

Asher brings with him over forty years of working as a CPA, with a focus on tax planning and preparation, and business consulting. As a financial planner he specializes in trust, estate and retirement income planning. He has been a columnist for the *Jewish Press* on financial matters, has been an advocate for promoting financial literacy, especially among young adults, and has lectured in many schools and civic organizations.

He leads an inspired life rich in challenges and rewards. Away from the office, you'll find him with his family, reading, or at the Table Tennis Club (still playing after winning his collegiate table tennis doubles championship at the City University of New York) and is involved in charitable activities including serving on the boards of a number of charitable organizations.

Made in the USA
San Bernardino, CA
22 December 2015